Foreword

The Hidden Places series is a collection of easy to use travel guides taking you, in this instance, on a relaxed but informative tour through the county of Cheshire, an area of varied landscape and heritage. Our books contain a wealth of interesting information on the history, the countryside, the towns and villages and the more established places of interest in the county. But they also promote the more secluded and little known visitor attractions and places to stay, eat and drink many of which are easy to miss unless you know exactly where you are going.

We include hotels, inns, restaurants, public houses, teashops, various types of accommodation, historic houses, museums, gardens, garden centres, craft centres and many other attractions throughout Cheshire. Most places have an attractive line drawing and are cross-referenced to coloured maps found at the rear of the book. We do not award merit marks or rankings but concentrate on describing the more interesting, unusual or unique features of each place with the aim of making the reader's stay in the local area an enjoyable and stimulating experience.

Whether you are visiting the area for business or pleasure or in fact are living in the county we do hope that you enjoy reading and using this book. We are always interested in what readers think of places covered (or not covered) in our guides so please do not hesitate to use the reader reaction forms provided to give us your considered comments. We also welcome any general comments which will help us improve the guides themselves. Finally if you are planning to visit any other corner of the British Isles we would like to refer you to the list of other *Hidden Places* titles to be found at the rear of the book.

The
HIDDEN PLACES
of
CHESHIRE

including
The Wirral

Edited by
David Gerrard

1998© Travel Publishing Ltd. 1998

663002 J

Published by:
Travel Publishing Ltd
7a Apollo House, Calleva Park
Aldermaston, Berks, RG7 8TN

ISBN 1-902-00716-6
© Travel Publishing Ltd 1998

First Published:	*1989*
Second Edition:	*1990*
Third Edition:	*1993*
Fourth Edition:	*1995*
Fifth Edition:	*1998*

Regional Titles in the Hidden Places Series:

Channel Islands	Cheshire
Cornwall	Devon
Dorset, Hants & Isle of Wight	Gloucestershire
Heart of England	Kent
Lake District & Cumbria	Lancashire
Norfolk	Northeast Yorkshire
Northumberland & Durham	Nottinghamshire
Peak District	Potteries
Somerset	South East
South Wales	Suffolk
Surrey	Sussex
Thames & Chilterns	Welsh Borders
Wiltshire	Yorkshire Dales

National Titles in the Hidden Places Series:

England	Ireland
Scotland	Wales

Printing by: Nuffield Press, Abingdon

Cartography by: Estates Publications, Tenterden, Kent

Line Drawings: Sarah Bird

Editor: David Gerrard

Cover : Clare Hackney

Born in 1961, Clare was educated at West Surrey College of Art and Design
as well as studying at Kingston University. She runs her own private water-
colour school based in Surrey and has exhibited both in the UK and
internationally. The cover is taken from an original water-colour of Little
Moreton Hall, Congleton.

Contents

CHAPTER ONE
Chester and The Wirral

Ness Gardens

Chapter 1 - Area Covered

For precise location of places please refer to the colour maps found at the rear of the book.

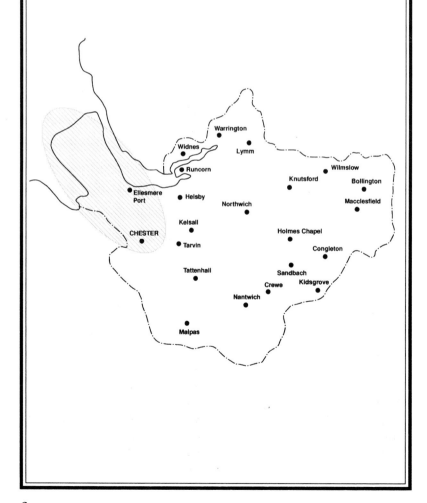

1
Chester & The Wirral

Introduction

Around the 1890s, guide-book writers took a fancy to describing the topography of various counties by comparing their outlines to some appropriate emblem. The hunting county of Leicestershire, for example, clearly resembled a fox's head with its ears pricked up. In Cheshire's county boundaries however they were unable to discern anything more imaginative than the shape of a teapot. Its base is the Staffordshire border, its handle the strip of land running from Stockport up to the Yorkshire border, with the Wirral providing the spout. And, tucked away at the base of the spout, is the capital of the county, the City of Chester.

The city's real position, a strategic site on the River Dee close to the Welsh border, was important even before the Romans arrived in AD70. They based a large camp, or *"caster"*, here and called it *Deva* after the Celtic name for the river. It was during this period that the splendid city walls were originally built - two miles round, and still the most complete in the country.

In Saxon times *"Ceastre"* became the administrative centre of a shire, and was the last major town in England to fall to William the Conqueror during his dreadful Harrowing of the North. William pulled down half of Chester's houses and reinforced the message of Norman domination by building a castle overlooking the Dee.

Subsequent Earls of Chester (the present Prince of Wales is the current one, incidentally) were given a free, and very firm hand, in dealing with the local Saxons and with the still-rebellious Welsh who continued to make a nuisance of themselves right through the

Middle Ages. In return for its no-nonsense dealing with these problems Chester received a number of royal privileges: borough status, a licence for a market and, around 1120, the first commission in England for a Sheriff, - long before his more famous colleague in Nottingham received his. The Mayor of Chester can still claim the medieval title of *"Admiral of the Dee"*.

The problem with the Welsh was finally resolved in 1485 when a Welsh-based family, the Tudors, defeated Richard III at Bosworth Field and Owen Tudor claimed the throne as Henry VII. For more than 150 years Chester enjoyed an unprecedented period of peace and prosperity. Then came the Civil War. Chester supported the King but Charles I had the galling experience of watching from the city walls as his troops were defeated at nearby Rowton Moor. For two long years after that rout, the city was under seige until starvation finally forced its capitulation. The *King Charles Tower* on the wall is now a small museum with displays telling the story of that siege.

Seventy years later, in the course of his *"Tour through the Whole Island of Great Britain"*, Daniel Defoe came to Chester by the ferry over the River Dee. He liked the city streets, *"very broad and fair"*; admired the *"very pleasant walk round the city, upon the walls"*, disliked its cathedral, *"built of red, sandy, ill looking stone"*, but had nothing but praise for its *"excellent cheese"*. Cheshire cheese had been fa-

King Charles Tower

mous for generations. John Speed, the famous Elizabethan map-maker and a Cheshire man himself, noted: *"The soil is fat fruitful and rich....the Pastures make the Kine's udders to strout to the pail, from whom the best Cheese of all Europe is made"*. Later, some enthusiasts even promoted the idea that the name Cheshire was actually short for cheese-shire.

The county's other major industry was salt, mined here even before the Romans arrived. By the time of the Domesday Book, the salt towns, or *"wiches"* - Nantwich, Northwich, Middlewich, were firmly established. The process then involved pumping the salt brine to the surface and boiling it to produce granular salt. In 1670, huge deposits of rock salt were discovered and these are still being mined, mostly for use in keeping the country's roads free from ice.

Both these historic industries have been overtaken in the 20th century by tourism. Chester, with its long history, varied and fascinating *"magpie"* architecture, and huge range of shops, restaurants and inns, is now the fourth most visited location in England after the *"golden triangle"* of London, Stratford and Oxford. One small disappointment, though. Visitors don't get to see the county's best known character, the grinning Cheshire Cat. The phrase *"To grin like a Cheshire cat"* was in use long before Lewis Carroll adopted it in Alice in Wonderland. Carroll spent his childhood in the Cheshire village of Daresbury and would have regularly seen the local cheeses moulded into various animal shapes, one of which was a grinning cat.

Chester

James Boswell, Dr Johnson's biographer, visited Chester in the 1770s and wrote "I was quite enchanted at Chester, so that I could with difficulty quit it". He was to return again, declaring that "Chester pleases my fancy more than any town I ever saw". Modern visitors will almost certainly share his enthusiasm.

Probably the best introduction to this compact little city is to join one of the frequent sightseeing tours conducted by a Blue Badge guide. These take place every day, even Christmas Day, and leave from the **Chester Visitor Centre**. The Centre can also provide you with a wealth of information about the city, including a full calendar of events that range from the **Chester Regatta**, the oldest rowing races in the world and **Chester Races**, the oldest in Britain, to the **Lord Mayor's Show** in May and the **Festival of Transport**, featuring an amazing parade of vintage cars, in August.

Towering above the city centre is **Chester Cathedral**, a majestic building of weathered pink stone which in 1992 celebrated its 900th birthday. It was originally an Abbey and is one of very few to survive Henry VIII's closure of the monasteries in the 1540s. The cloisters are regarded as the finest in England and the monks' refectory is still serving food although nowadays it is refreshments and lunches for visitors. It was at Chester Cathedral, in 1742, that George Frederick Handel personally conducted rehearsals of his oratorio "The Messiah" before its first performance in Dublin: a copy of the score with annotations in his own hand remains on display.

Chester Cathedral

Chester is famous for its outstanding range of museums, from the **Deva Roman Experience** where you can re-live the sights, sounds and even the smells of daily Roman life, through the **Grosvenor Museum** with its furnished period rooms, to the **Chester Heritage Centre** which tells the city's story from the Civil War siege to the present day. **On The Air** broadcasting museum chronicles the world of radio and television from the pioneering days of BBC radio to satellite TV, while the **Chester Toy & Doll Museum** is a nostalgic treasure-house of antique playthings

Quite apart from its historical attractions, Chester is also one of the major shopping centres for the north west and north Wales. All the familiar High Street names are here, often housed in much more appealing buildings than they usually inhabit, along with a great number of specialist and antique shops. For a unique shopping experience, you must visit the world-famous, two-tiered galleries of shops under covered walkways known as *The Rows* which line both sides of Bridge Street. The Rows are an architectural one-off: no other medieval town has anything like them. Many of the black and white, half-timbered frontages of The Rows, so typical of Chester and Cheshire, are actually Victorian restorations, but crafted so beautifully and faithfully that even experts can have difficulty distinguishing them from their 13th century originals.

The Rows, Chester

Close by is the *Eastgate Clock*. It was erected in 1897 to celebrate Queen Victoria's Diamond Jubilee, a beautifully ornate construction which is probably the most photographed timepiece in the world. If your timing is right and you arrive hereabouts at 12 noon in the summer, you should see, and certainly hear, the *Town Crier* delivering some stentorian civic message.

A few steps bring you to Chester's famous **City Walls** which were originally built by the Romans to protect the fortress of Deva from attacks by pesky Celtic tribes. Nowadays, the two-mile long circuit, - an easy, level promenade, provides thousands of visitors with some splendid views of the River Dee, of the city's many glorious buildings and of the distant Welsh mountains. Here, during the summer months, you may come across Caius Julius Quartus, a **Roman Legionary Officer** in shining armour conducting a patrol around the fortress walls and helping to re-create the life and times of a frontline defender of the Empire. At one point, the wall runs alongside St John Street, which has a curious history. In Roman times it was the main thoroughfare between the fortress and the **Amphitheatre**, the largest ever uncovered in Britain, capable of seating 7,000 spectators. During the Middle Ages however this highway was excavated and turned into a defensive ditch. Over the years, the ditch gradually filled up and by Elizabethan times St John Street was a proper street once again.

The heart of the old city is now reserved for pedestrians only and Foregate Street is part of this walker-friendly area. Here you'll find **Ryan's Irish Bar.** It's housed in what used to be a pharmacy and the old chemist's magnificent medicine cabinet is still in place with its multiplicity of shelves and drawers where drugs and various potions were stored. Nowadays, potions of a much more palatable kind are dispensed in this lively, open-plan pub, although there are other mementoes of its former history in the vintage instruments and artefacts displayed inside wood and glass columns. Excellent food is served, at lunchtimes only, and the menu naturally includes some Irish choices such as Guinness & Stilton pâté,

Ryan's Irish Bar

Irish Stew, and Irish Cream Bash for dessert, along with a good choice of traditional English pub dishes.

There's a Hibernian flavour evident too in the selection of beers, amongst them Kilkenny, Irish Harp and Guinness. And the Irish theme is enhanced even more on Sunday evenings when live bands play both traditional and contemporary Irish music. *Ryan's Irish Bar, 98, Foregate Street, Chester, CH1 1JB. Tel: 01244 319813*

Rivers always add a special attraction to a city and Chester certainly makes good use of the River Dee. Rowing boats, motor boats, canoes, are all available for hire, and comfortable cruisers offer sightseeing tours along the river as far as the Crook of Dee, opposite the Duke of Westminster's stately residence of Eaton Hall.

Many of these boats depart from The Groves, close to Maggie Warrington's *Riverside Café & Tea Gardens* which enjoys a superb position on the bank of the river. Housed in a grand old Victorian

Riverside Café & Tea Gardens

property, and with a large patio and terraces outside, the Riverside Café has been one of Chester's best known and most popular tea rooms for more than half a century. The beautiful location, the friendly waitress service and excellent fare have all contributed to its continuing success.

Light meals are available all day, and so is the set tea which includes a pot of tea, choice of sandwich, buttered scone, cream and jam. Also extremely popular is Maggie's lunchtime special which always begins with a steaming bowl of home-made soup and is served from noon until 2.30pm. Easily reached on foot from the city centre, a visit to the Riverside Café is an experience not to be missed. It is open every day, all year, until 9pm in the season, around 5pm at other times. *Riverside Café & Tea Gardens, The Groves, Chester. Tel: 01244 314440*

The Beehive in Flookersbrook is definitely the right kind of pub for people who are very discriminating about their ale, enjoy a sociable game of pool, snooker or darts, and above all, a warm and friendly atmosphere. The decoration in Judy Bennett's popular inn reflects its customers' priorities with large mirrors, posters, and beer towels all advertising famous beverages. About 150 years old, The Beehive is primarily a wet pub but Judy also serves a small selection of filled rolls, sandwiches and pies.

The Beehive

There's live entertainment every Saturday evening, sometimes on Fridays as well, and there's always a good crowd around the giant TV screen for any major sporting event. There are special prices for double measures of spirits throughout the day and Judy has also introduced a privilege card scheme for regulars which can be used to obtain special discounts off ales advertised on the blackboard. The Beehive is open all day, every day: children though are not admitted at any time. *The Beehive, 15, Hoole Road, Flookersbrook, Chester, CH2 3NH. Tel: 01244 354091*

Established twenty years ago **Grosvenor Garden Centre** is known as Chester's Premier Garden Centre. Extending over fourteen acres, all of them bursting with ideas for your garden and house, there is a wonderful display of plants, trees, shrubs, herbaceous, alpines and bedding. The two-year guarantee on hardy container-grown plants is a clear indication of Grosvenor's confidence in the quality of their plants. Garden Accessories include garden lighting and furniture, water fountains, stoneware and wind chimes. Grosvenor offers what

Grosvenor Garden Centre

is probably the largest display of containers in the area. Tubs, pots, troughs, made of terracotta, stone, wood, ceramics and plastic (including some Ali Baba-sized terracotta pots), - you will be spoilt for choice. There is a superior and stylish giftware department with the latest designs from the continent. a wonderful floristry area and the books and crafts department more than caters for children.

There is an excellent cafe, The Orangery, which overlooks the plant area and children's play area while you enjoy a hot meal, a tasty snack and a cup of excellent tea or coffee. Other facilities are aquatic fish and plants, fresh flowers and bouquets, conservatories, sheds and greenhouses, and the best selection of tents and camping equipment in the area. It's impossible to list all Grosvenor's features - you should really go and take a look for yourself. *Grosvenor Garden Centre, Wrexham Road, Belgrave, Chester CH4 9EB. Tel: 01244 682856*

Built in the mid-19th century, **The Engine House Tavern** looks over the road to the River Dee, Chester city centre is just a ten minute walk away, and the historic church of St Paul's with its lepers' graveyard and martyr's memorial stands close by. The tavern's unusual name has nothing to do with railway engines but comes from the pumping engine a short distance away that extracted wa-

The Engine House Tavern

ter from the Dee and propelled it to the Chester Waterworks. This popular pub, run by Michael and Janet, has a strong emphasis on games, with darts and pool matches on most weekday evenings. At the time of going to press, the Engine House Tavern is a wet pub only but plans are under way to start serving bar snacks at lunchtime, along with evening quizzes and entertainment. Ale is taken seriously here and those on offer include Youngers, John Smiths, Theakstons and Beamish. The tavern is open every day from noon-3pm, and from 7pm-11pm (Sundays, 10.30pm). *The Engine House Tavern, 111, Boughton, Chester, CH3 5BH. 01244 344706*

No visit to Chester would be complete without a trip to **Chester Zoo** on the northern edge of the city. Set in 110 acres of landscaped gardens, it's the largest zoo in Britain, caring for more than 5000 animals from some 500 different species. The Zoo also provides a refuge for many rare and endangered animals which breed freely in near-natural enclosures. What's more, it has the UK's largest elephant facility and is the only successful breeder of Asiatic elephants in this country. Offering more than enough interest for a full day out, the Zoo is open every day of the year except Christmas Day.

Tarvin
Map 1 ref D5

5 miles E of Chester off the A54

One fortunate result of the major fire that destroyed much of Tarvin in 1752 was that the rebuilding of the village left it with an abundance of handsome Georgian buildings. **The George & Dragon** in the High Street is one of them. A fascinating feature of the interior of the inn is the huge mural which covers the whole of one wall and depicts the village as it was in the 19th century. By that time, The George & Dragon had already been dispensing hospitality for more than a hundred years, and another century later, it still is. Mel and Karen Corrall run this impressive old hostelry with its twin bay windows, tubs of colourful flowers, and an interior full of character

The George & Dragon

and charm. Choosing your food here is a serious matter. Karen's menu runs to ten pages, starting with home made soup and, more than 150 choices later, offering you Death by White Chocolate. You'll find just about everything you can think of on this list - from hearty 8oz steaks, through the Italian speciality of filled Bughy Bughy Bread, to a simple tuna roll for around a £1. As if that weren't enough, Mel and Karen also offer a series of entertainments: karaoke (the first Saturday evening of each month); music nights (the first Thursday of each month); horse racing nights every three months; and a quiz night every Thursday. *The George & Dragon, 67, High Street, Tarvin, nr Chester, CH3 8EE. Tel: 01829 741446*

Grove House is a grand old Victorian house whose bed and breakfast accommodation has had tourist authorities, travel guides and writers queueing up to present it with awards. (The AA's 5 Qs accolade was amongst the most recent). It seems that anyone who stays at John and Helen Spiegelberg's beautifully-furnished home, surrounded by 1½ acres of its own beautiful grounds, wants to pin a medal on their hosts. The walled garden, the venerable old trees, many of them listed, the croquet lawn, all contribute to the charm of staying at Grove House, as do the spacious and comfortable rooms, each one fully equipped with such amenities as colour television and tea/coffee making facilities.

Grove House

There are three letting rooms: a king-sized en suite, a twin en suite, and a double with its own private bathroom. If you prefer a continental breakfast, it can be served in your room: the full English version awaits you downstairs. So if you are planning to stay anywhere in the Chester area - the historic city is just five miles away - think first of Grove House. And don't forget to bring your own medal ready to bestow! *Grove House, Holme Street, Tarvin, Chester, CH3 8EQ. Tel: 01829 740893*

The Wirral

Two Old English words meaning heathland covered with bog myrtle gave The Wirral its name and well into modern times it was a byword for a desolate place. The 14th century author of *"Sir Gawayne and the Green Knight"* writes of:

> *"The wilderness of Wirral: few lived there*
> *Who loved with a good heart either God or man"*

The Wirral's inhabitants were infamous for preying on the ship-wrecks tossed on to its marshy coastline by gales sweeping off the

Irish Sea. The 19th century development of shipbuilding at Birkenhead brought industry on a large scale to the Mersey shore but also an influx of prosperous Liverpool commuters who colonised the villages of the Caldy and Grange Hills and transformed the former wilderness into a leafy suburbia. The 1974 Local Government changes handed two thirds of The Wirral to Merseyside leaving Cheshire with by far the most attractive third, the southern and western parts alongside the River Dee. Tourism officials now refer to The Wirral as the *"Leisure Peninsula"*, a fair description of this

Ness Gardens, Neston

appealing and comparatively little-known area. One of its major attractions is **Ness Gardens**, a 64-acre tract of superbly landscaped gardens on the banks of the River Dee. The gardens are run by the University of Liverpool as an Environmental and Horticultural Research Station and are planned to provide magnificent displays all year round. There are children's play and picnic areas, and well-marked interest trails, and licensed refreshment rooms.

Neston   Map 1 ref B3
11 miles NW of Chester off the A540

Right up until the early 19th century, Neston was the most significant town in The Wirral, one of the string of small ports along the River Dee. In Tudor times, Neston had been one of the main embarkation points for travellers to Ireland but the silting up of the river was so swift and inexorable that by the time the New Quay, begun in 1545, was completed, it had became useless. Visiting Neston in the late 1700s, Anna Seward described the little town set on a hill overlooking the Dee Estuary as *"a nest from the storm of the ocean"*.

At the time Anna visited Neston, **The Brewers Arms** was a substantial farmhouse, already more than a hundred years old, but not yet the warm and inviting hostelry it is today. This lovely old pub has been run by Gwen and Ian Hamilton since 1989 and its popularity owes a lot to their engaging personalities, - the excellent food

The Brewers Arms

they serve may also have something to do with it. Whether you fancy a hearty steak, a crisp salad, a fish or vegetarian meal, just a light snack, filled baguette or a sandwich, you will find it on the menu, along with a Kiddies Corner list of dishes for the under-12s. Daily specials add to the choice. The Brewers Arms also offers its customers a wide range of entertainment: Country & Western music on Sundays, traditional jazz on Mondays, pool on Tuesdays, and Quizzes on Wednesdays and Thursdays. *The Brewers Arms, 1, Park Street, Neston, South Wirral, L64 3RP. Tel: 0151 336 1627*

Parkgate   *Map 1 ref B3*
12 miles NW of Chester via the A540 and B5134

After Neston port became unusable, maritime traffic moved along the Dee Estuary to Parkgate which, as the new gateway to Ireland, saw some notable visitors. John Wesley, who made regular trips to Ireland, preached here while waiting for a favourable wind, and George Frederick Handel returned via Parkgate after conducting the first performance of *"The Messiah"* in Dublin. J.M.W. Turner came to sketch the lovely view across to the Flintshire hills. A little later, Parkgate enjoyed a brief spell as a fashionable spa. Lord Nelson's mistress, Lady Hamilton (who was born at nearby Neston) took the waters here in an effort to cure an unfortunate skin disease, another visitor was Mrs Fitzherbert, already secretly married to the Prince Regent, later George IV. When Holyhead developed into the main gateway to Ireland, Parkgate's days as a port and watering-place were numbered. But with fine Georgian houses lining the promenade, this attractive little place still retains the atmosphere of a gracious spa town

The Ship Hotel enjoys a marvellous position on The Parade with magnificent views across the Dee Estuary to the North Wales countryside. This friendly, informal hotel is ideally placed for exploring the Wirral coastline and its wealth of attractions. And how pleasant to return after a day's sightseeing to The Ship's open fires, flagstone floors, even perhaps to one of its four poster beds. The restaurant here has a great reputation locally for its good food, fine

The Ship Hotel

wines, excellent service, and an extensive menu that caters for every taste. Hot and cold food is also available in the bar at lunchtimes and evenings every day. The Ship has 26 letting rooms, ~ singles, doubles, triples, all with private bathroom and furnished with every amenity. There's a Quiz on Wednesday evenings, live music on Sunday nights, and The Ship also offers some extremely attractive rates for week and weekend breaks, ~ complete with a 3-course candlelit dinner. *The Ship Inn, The Parade, Parkgate, South Wirral, L64 6SA. Tel: 0151 336 3931*

The Marsh Cat

Andy Wareham and Phil Williams only opened **The Marsh Cat** at Parkgate in November 1997 but their superb restaurant has already been showered with praise. The views across the Dee estuary would in themselves make a visit worthwhile, but it is the outstanding food served here that has attracted rave reviews from the many newspaper and magazine food writers who have come to sample Phil's cuisine. Phil was born in Belize, trained in New Orleans, and in the course of some twenty-odd years experience as a chef has garnered an astonishing collection of awards and medals for his cooking. His menus change frequently but always include some less familiar dishes from around the world. So, along with the rack of English lamb in a herb scented crust, or the Venison Juniper, you might also find on offer Moules Thailandaise, Louisiana Seafood Gumbo or a Mexican Chargrilled Quesadilla.

The Marsh Cat is open for lunch and dinner every day and such is the restaurant's popularity bookings are advisable at all times and essential at weekends. There's no space here to tell the tale of the Marsh Cat but you'll find the full story illustrated around the walls of this exceptional restaurant. *The Marsh Cat, 1, Mostyn Square, Parkgate, South Wirral, L64 6SL. Tel: 0151 336 1963*

Thornton Hough   *Map 1 ref B3*
14 miles NW of Chester via the A540 and B5136
The huge village green at Thornton Hough, covering some 14 acres and surrounded by half-timbered black and white houses, is one of

the most picturesque spots in Cheshire. Overlooking this lovely green is **The Seven Stars Inn**, built in the 1870s to provide light refreshment for travellers using the toll bridge nearby, and still offering traditional hospitality more than a century and a quarter later. With its decorative beams, inglenook fireplace, its collection of antique water jugs, and absence of juke boxes or fruit machines, The Seven

The Seven Stars Inn

Stars Inn is the epitome of the traditional English pub - except that the food is much better here! Mine hosts, David and Mary Jay show a genuine concern for their customers' comfort and enjoyment. There's a note on the menu, for example, asking you not to feel restricted by its contents: "If you would like anything which is not shown, let us know and if we have the ingredients we will try and make it for you". *The Seven Stars Inn, Thornton Hough, Wirral, L63 1JW. Tel: 0151 336 4574*

With its very distinctive tower, crowned by a witches-hat turret, **The Village Stores & Tearooms** at Thornton Hough provides an attractive and unusual location in which to enjoy a light lunch or afternoon tea. In the bright first-floor tea rooms, owner Angela Fisher offers visitors an appetising selection of home made cakes and pies, savouries and snacks, and a special hot dish of the day. The tea room has a notable reputation for serving excellent Douwe Egbert's coffee, and Twining's tea, in delicate bone china. If you plan to visit on a Saturday afternoon, you would be well advised to make a booking. Downstairs, Angela has converted the ground floor into a showroom where you'll find a fascinating mix: antique and decorative textiles, intriguing examples of furniture made from Lincolnshire potato baskets, teddy bears made of German mohair, and much more. If you are a devotee of teddy bears, you will also want to visit Angela's shop in Brimstage, just a mile away, which deals exclusively with the cuddly creatures and with all the accessories they need to make them happy. *The Village Stores & Tearooms, Thornton Common Road, Thornton Hough, Wirral, L63 1JL. Tel: 0151 336 3719*

The Village Stores & Tearooms

Willaston-in-Wirral

Map 1 ref B3

10 miles NW of Chester via the A540 and B5151

Hadlow Road Station, a short distance from the centre of Willaston, hasn't seen a train since 1962. But everything here is spick and span, the signal box and ticket office apparently ready for action, a trolley laden with milk churns waiting on the platform. Restored to appear as it would have done on a typical day in 1952, the station is an intriguing feature on the **Wirral Way**. This 12 mile long linear nature reserve follows the track of the old railway between Hooton and West Kirkby and was, in 1973, one of the first Country Parks to be opened.

Just outside Willaston, on Benty Heath Lane, you will find the **Raby House Hotel**. This very attractive and impressive red brick mansion in Jacobean style was originally built in 1867 as a private house for the Johnson family of the Liverpool Shipping Line. Set in lovely countryside with breathtaking views in all directions, Raby House is very much a family run business, with Sean McKenna the third generation of his family to care for this beautifully-located

The Raby House Hotel

hotel. His mum and dad, Val and Rob, are also actively involved in ensuring that the hotel maintains its superlative reputation for good food and accommodation. Sean takes personal charge of the kitchen, and offers very reasonably priced bar meals as well as an extensive à la carte menu served in the Raby House Restaurant where you'll also find a distinguished list of wines from around the world. The hotel is licensed for civil marriages and can provide a comprehensive package for the special day: a large function room, excellent catering, ideal grounds for wedding photographs, and a choice of no fewer than three bridal suites. *The Raby House Hotel, Benty Heath Lane, Willaston-in-Wirral, L64 1SB. Tel: 0151 327 1900*

Eastham   *Map 1 ref C3*
10 miles NW of Chester off the A41

Eastham Woods Country Park is a 76-acre oasis of countryside amidst industrial Merseyside and enjoys considerable status amongst bird-watchers as one of few northern woodlands with all three species of native woodpecker in residence. Just a mile or so from the Park is Eastham village, another little oasis with a church and old houses grouped around the village green. The venerable yew tree in the churchyard is reputed to be the oldest in England.

CHAPTER TWO
South Cheshire & the Welsh Borders

Nantwich

Chapter 2 - Area Covered

*For precise location of places please refer to the colour
maps found at the rear of the book.*

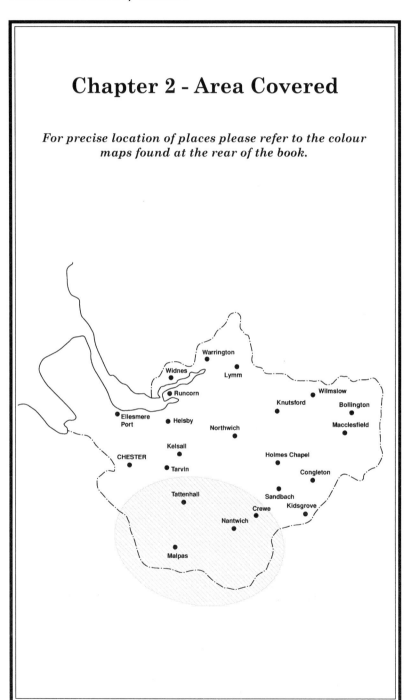

2
South Cheshire & the Welsh Borders

South Cheshire

The two major towns of South Cheshire are *Nantwich*, with a history stretching back beyond Roman times, and *Crewe*, with no history at all until 1837. That was when the Grand Junction Railway arrived and five years later moved all its construction and repair workshops to this green field site. A workforce of nine hundred had to be housed so the company rapidly built cottages, each one shared by four of the lowest paid workers, and detached *"mansions"* which accommodated four families of the more highly skilled. Later, in 1887, the railway company also provided the town with one of the most splendid parks in the north of England, *Queens Park*, some 40 acres of lawns and flowerbeds together with an ornamental lake. Rolls Royce's engineering works brought further prosperity to the town, but it is as a railway centre that Crewe is best known. Even today, the station offers a choice of six different routes to all points of the compass. *The Railway Age* museum offers a fascinating insight into Crewe's place in railway history with hands-on exhibits, steam locomotive rides, model railway displays and a children's playground. Also worth a visit is the *Lyceum Theatre*, built in 1902 and with its glorious Edwardian opulence undimmed.

Nantwich

The most disastrous event in the long history of Nantwich was the Great Fire of 1583 which consumed some 600 of its thatched and timber-framed buildings. The blaze raged for 20 days and the terror of the townspeople was compounded when some bears kept behind the Crown Hotel escaped. (Four bears from Nantwich are mentioned in Shakespeare's comedy *"The Merry Wives of Windsor"*). Queen Elizabeth contributed the huge sum of £2000 and also donated quantities of timber from Delamere Forest to assist in the town's rebuilding. A grateful citizen, Thomas Cleese, commemorated this royal largesse with a plaque on his new house at No. 41, High Street. The plaque is still in place and reads:

> *"God grant our ryal Queen in England longe to raign*
> *For she hath put her helping hand to bild this towne again".*

The most striking of the buildings to survive the conflagration, perhaps because it was surrounded by a moat, is the lovely black and white house in Hospital Street, known as ***Churche's Mansion*** after the merchant Richard Churche who built it in 1577. Astonishingly, when the house was up for sale in 1930, no buyer showed any interest and the building was on the point of being transported brick by brick to America when a public-spirited local doctor stepped in and rescued it. The ground floor is now a restaurant, but the upper floor has been furnished in Elizabethan style and is open to the public during the summer.

Churche's Mansion

The Great Fire also spared the stone-built 14th century church. This fine building, with an unusual octagonal tower, is sometimes called the **Cathedral of South Cheshire** and dates from the period of the town's greatest prosperity as a salt town and trading centre. Of exceptional interest is the magnificent chancel and the wonderful carvings in the choir. On the misericords (tip-up seats) are mermaids, foxes (some dressed as monks in a sharp dig at priests), pigs, and the legendary Wyvern, half-dragon, half-bird, whose name is linked with the River Weaver, 'wyvern' being an old pronunciation of Weaver. An old tale about the building of the church tells of an old woman who brought ale and food each day from a local inn to the masons working on the site. The masons discovered that the woman was cheating them by keeping back some of the money they put *"in the pot"* for their refreshment. They dismissed her and took revenge by making a stone carving showing the old woman being carried away by Old Nick himself, her hand still stuck in a pot.

Nantwich

During the Civil War, Nantwich was the only town in Cheshire to support Cromwell's Parliamentary army. After several weeks of fighting, the Royalist forces were finally defeated on 25th January, 1644 and the people of Nantwich celebrated by wearing sprigs of holly in their hair. As a result, the day became known as *"Holly Holy Day"* and every year, on the Saturday closest to January 25th, the town welcomes Cromwellian pikemen and battle scenes are re-enacted by members of the Sealed Knot. There are records of the Civil War in the **Nantwich Museum** in Pillory Street which also has exhibitions about the town and its dairy and cheese-making industries.

But it was salt that had once made Nantwich second only in importance to Chester in the county. The Romans had mined salt here for their garrisons at Chester and Stoke where the soldiers received part of their wages in *"sal"*, or salt. The payment was called a *"salarium"*, hence the modern word salary. Nantwich remained a salt producing town right up to the 18th century but then it was overtaken by towns like Northwich which enjoyed better communications on the canal system. But a brine spring still supplies Nantwich's outdoor swimming pool!

At **Fields Farm Cottages**, surrounded by open Cheshire countryside, it's difficult to believe that you are just a few minutes drive from the busy centre of Nantwich. The Shropshire Union Canal passes to the west of the farm, offering pleasant towpath walks; other paths lead into Nantwich, skirting the River Weaver. On this

Fields Farm Cottages

57 acre farm, David Heys offers two pretty cottages, both available all year and each providing accommodation for up to six people. Beautifully converted about six years ago from former shippons (cowsheds) and a pig sty, the cottages are attractively furnished in country style and both have large living rooms one of which doubles up as a kitchen/dining-room. The kitchens are well-equipped with every mod. con. (including a microwave) and there's also a shared utility room with washer-dryer, ironing facilities, and a pay phone. Children, and disabled people accompanied by a carer, are very welcome. *Fields Farm Cottages, Edleston, Nantwich, CW5 5JL. Tel: 01270 625769*

Willaston

Map 2 ref F7

2 miles E of Nantwich between the A534 and A500

It was in the village of Willaston that one of the most unusual world records was established in 1994. Some 200 competitors had gathered at the Primary School here for the annual **World Worm Charming Championships**. The prize goes to whoever induces the greatest number of worms to poke their heads above a square metre of soil. Each contestant is allowed fifteen minutes and the current world champion charmed his worms out at the rate of more than ten a minute. His wonderful way with worms remains a secret.

Willaston can also take pride in its pub. For years, Terry and Marilyn Manning cherished the ambition of taking over their favourite local, **The Horse Shoe Inn**, a short drive from the centre of historic Nantwich. In July 1997, their dream came true and they now happily preside over these attractive old premises which, in their time, have served as a brewery, a smithy, and an alehouse before finding their proper role as an inviting pub.

Here, Terry and Marilyn offer an hospitable welcome, fine, well-kept ales and a tasty choice of main meals, snacks, sweets and children's menu along with a blackboard list of daily specials. The Horse Shoe Inn's large garden, patio and children's play area make this an ideal place for family visits. This busy inn is now very much

The Horse Shoe Inn

a social centre for Willaston offering, amongst other activities, a thriving Golf Society, a formidable domino team (of which both Terry and Marilyn are members), and a Quiz Night every Tuesday, starting at 9.30pm. The Mannings' delight in having their long-held ambition realised will be shared by anyone visiting this popular, lively pub. *The Horse Shoe Inn, Newcastle Road, Willaston, Nantwich, CW5 7EP. Tel: 01270 569404*

Wybunbury

Map 2 ref G7

4 miles SE of Nantwich on the B5071

South Cheshire's answer to the Leaning Tower of Pisa is the 100ft high tower of **St Chad's Church** in Wybunbury. It was built in 1470 above an unsuspected ancient salt bed. Subsidence has been the reason for the tower's long history of leaning sideways by as much as four feet and then being straightened up, most recently in 1989. It now rests on a reinforced concrete bed and is unlikely to deviate from the vertical again. The tower stands alone: the body of the church, once capable of holding a congregation of 1600, collapsed on no fewer than five occasions. In 1972, the villagers finally decided to abandon it and build a new church on firmer ground.

Enjoying a prime location close to St Chad's is **The Swan Inn**, one of the most attractive buildings in this pretty village. The inn's history goes back to the 1500s and the old beams inside evoke a powerful flavour of those bygone days. The Swan is owned and run by Malcolm and Sandra Groom who came here in 1995 and already have a roaring success on their hands. Excellent food is available every lunchtime and evening (booking advisable at weekends), eve-

The Swan Inn

rything cooked to order, served in generous portions and at very reasonable prices. The selection includes hearty main courses, salads, ploughman's and sandwiches. For beer-drinkers, there's always a choice of at least six different bitters. Outside, a large patio looks over to the village's famous *"leaning tower"*, and the old outbuildings have been charmingly converted into 7 en suite letting rooms, each with lots of space, large bathrooms and lovely views across the countryside. *The Swan Inn, Main Road, Wybunbury, CW5 7NE. Tel: 01270 841280*

Hunsterson   *Map 2 ref G7*
5 miles SE of Nantwich on minor road between A529 and A51

About five miles out of Nantwich, ***Foxes Bank Farm Caravan Park*** enjoys a splendid, west-facing position, ideal for a peaceful evening drink. Foxes Bank Farm is a 130-acre working dairy and sheep farm, set in attractive countryside close to the long-distance walk, the South Cheshire Way. In fact, there's quite a network of

Foxes Bank Farm Caravan Park

walks nearby and Judy Rees, who owns the caravan park with her husband David, has set up her own information cabin here providing details of these routes and of other attractions in the neighbourhood.

Very much a family business, with son Timothy and daughter-in-law Rachel also involved, Foxes Bank opened in 1992. Today, the 1½ acre site has pitches for 15 tourers, (each with its own electricity hook-up point), and a well-equipped toilet and shower block. Children are welcome and so are dogs on leads. This well-run site provides an excellent base from which to explore south Cheshire, with Staffordshire, Shropshire and even north Wales all within easy reach. *Foxes Bank Farm Caravan Park, Hunsterson, nr Nantwich, CW5 7PN. Tel: 01270 520224*

Newtown & Broomhall
Map 2 ref F7
3 miles S of Nantwich on the A530
Close to the village of Newtown and hidden away in the small village of Broomhall is **Lane Farm Antiques**, well worth seeking out. To find it, take the A530 from Nantwich to Whitchurch and, when you come to Broomhall village, look for Heatley Lane on your left. Turn here and, about a couple of hundred yards on your left, is Glyn

Lane Farm Antiques

and Jayne Tatler's antique shop specialising in furniture from every age, and in a multiplicity of styles. Anything old, well-made and well-designed justifies its place here, providing a range of attractive pieces that includes beds, tables, wardrobes, - indeed any item of furniture that might add a distinctive touch to your home. Much of it is of English origin, but you'll also find interesting items from Belgium and Holland along with some unusual pieces made from East German pine. Lane Farm Antiques is normally open during regular shop hours, but if you are making a special journey it's a good idea to telephone first. *Lane Farm Antiques, Lane Farm, Heatley Lane, Broomhall, Nantwich, CW5 8BA. Tel: 01270 780092*

Barbridge

Map 2 ref F6

4 miles NW of Nantwich on the A51

The Barbridge Inn enjoys an idyllic setting beside the Shropshire Union Canal, a perfect spot from which to watch the colourful narrow-boats and other pleasure craft passing by. The pub is as old as the canal which first opened back in the mid-18th century and 24-hour mooring is still available right outside. Mo and Bill Eyre run

The Barbridge Inn

this delightful inn which has a character all of its own. Guests will find an interesting and diverse menu, available either in the dining-room overlooking the canal or at the picnic tables outside, and a full range of ales, premium lagers, and wines from around the world. In the large canalside garden there's a children's play area and barbecues are often held here in summer. And for a gentle stroll after your meal, the canal towpath is ideal. This very special place can be found a few miles north of Nantwich, just off the A51 road to Chester. *The Barbridge Inn, Old Chester Road, Barbridge, nr Nantwich, CW5 6AY. Tel: 01270 528443*

Wardle

Map 2 ref F6

5 miles NW of Nantwich on the A51

The Jolly Tar Inn stands alongside the A51 at Wardle, just across the road from the junction of two historic canals, the Shropshire Union and the Middlewich Branch. There's been a pub here for many

The Jolly Tar Inn

years: the stylish, modern building now in place was opened in 1962. The Jolly Tar's popular hosts, Drew and Jane McCall, have plans to add a large conservatory, so adding another attraction to the inn's many amenities which include an extensive garden, patio and children's play area. In summer, the garden also offers a kids bouncy castle and barbecues on Fridays and Bank Holidays.

Inside, the inn is decorated with a nautical theme, dominated by a splendid ship's wheel, and there are many original paintings by local artists on display. The extensive menu, available every lunchtime and evening (except Tuesday lunchtimes in winter) offers an excellent choice of main dishes, lite bites and sandwiches, along with vegetarian options. This understandably popular pub also lays on live entertainment on Wednesday evenings, occasional quiz nights, and a Children in Need auction in November. *The Jolly Tar Inn, Nantwich Road, Wardle, CW5 6BE. Tel: 01270 528283*

Tattenhall

Map 2 ref D6

8 miles SE of Chester off the A41

Tattenhall is a fine old village within sight of the twin castles of Beeston and Peckforton perched atop the Peckforton Hills. There are some attractive old houses and a Victorian church with a graveyard which gained notoriety during the 19th century because of the activities of a gang of grave-robbers. They lived in caves in the hills nearby and, once they had disposed of the bodies to medical gentlemen, used the empty coffins to store their booty from more conventional thieving.

At that time Tattenhall was a busy little place. **The Shropshire Union Canal** passed close by and the village was served by two railway stations on different lines. Today, only one railway line survives (and no stations), the canal is used solely by pleasure craft, but the village is enjoying a new lease of life as a desirable community for people commuting to Chester, a short drive away.

Small though it is, Tattenhall has entertained some distinguished visitors. No less a personage than King James I once stayed at *The Bear & Ragged Staff*. This attractive hostelry was then a modest one-storey building with a thatched roof. It later became an important coaching inn, (the old mounting steps still stand outside), and in Victorian times acquired a second storey. In summer, The Bear & Ragged Staff looks particularly inviting with its hanging baskets

The Bear & Ragged Staff

and large beer garden at the back complete with bouncy castle, barbecues on Saturdays, and Fun Days once a month. The pub's unusual name suggests some connection with the Earls of Warwick whose crest it is. (The first Earl supposedly strangled a bear, the second Earl clubbed a giant to death). Roy and Sue Hankey run this appealing inn with its open fires and cobbled courtyard, and offer their visitors a good choice of "pub grub" and well-kept ales. They also lay on live entertainment every other Saturday, and a quiz night every other Sunday. *The Bear & Ragged Staff, High Street, Tattenhall, CH3 9PX. Tel: 01829 770308*

One of the best things about the British Empire was that it introduced us to some wonderful, exotic cuisines. Above all, we discovered a taste for the spicy, aromatic dishes of India, exactly the kind of food that Mr and Mrs Julani offer at *The Village Indian* restaurant in Tattenhall. From the outside, Clifden House is a typical Cheshire black and white building, but inside the decoration and furnishings have a sumptuous Oriental flavour.

The Village Indian Restaurant

The extensive menu specialises mainly in the cuisine of northern India, all wonderfully prepared by the Julanis who have more than twenty years experience in catering. Their menu also includes Thai, Indonesian and Bangladeshi dishes, and if you give them advance warning, the Julanis will even cook English food for you. Children can have half portions, the restaurant is equally divided between smoking and non-smoking areas, and on Sundays from 1pm until 5pm there's a lunch buffet where customers are invited to help themselves to as much as they can eat from a wide selection of exotic dishes. The restaurant is open every evening from 6pm to 11pm and, for serious lovers of Indian food, an essential date for the diary is the first Monday of every month: that is when The Village Indian holds its special gourmet evenings. *The Village Indian, Clifden House, High Street, Tattenhall, CH3 9PX. Tel: 01829 770839*

Gatesheath

Map 2 ref D6

8 miles SE of Chester of the A41

Occupying a Victorian farmhouse in Gatesheath, **The Country Centre** is a quite unique attraction. To begin with, there's the Orchard Paddock, a magnet for children with its appealing collection of farm animals and pets, swings and crazy golf. Anyone interested in flower arranging can watch the staff of the Dried Flower Workshop creating unique arrangements which can be bought, or you can buy all

The Country Centre

the materials to make your own. You can also see them creating painted plant pots, boxes and small pieces of furniture. There is a comprehensive display of greeting cards and gifts, and a tea room serving freshly brewed teas, coffee and home cooked food: what more can you want? Well, how about Uncle Peter's Fudge Kitchen where you can try the superbly tasty fudge made daily from the purest ingredients Incidentally, the name of the farm, New Russia Hall, has nothing to do with Muscovy or the *"Evil Empire"* but comes from a corruption of *"rushes"* which once grew abundantly in the marshy ground nearby and provided the basic materials for local basketmakers. *The Country Centre, New Russia Hall, Chester Rd, Gatesheath, nr Tattenhall, CH3 9AH. Tel: 01829 770901*

Huxley

Map 2 ref D5

8 miles SE of Chester on minor road between A41 and A51

How many bed and breakfast places in the country can trace their history back to the Domesday Book? **Higher Huxley Hall** can. At that time, more than 900 years ago, the Hall was a moated and fortified sandstone house. It was rebuilt in brick in the 14th century, enlarged in Elizabethan times, and further extended in the 1780s. The Marks family have lived in this historic house since the 1960s and run the 200-acre farm which has been continuously cultivated for some eight hundred years now.

Higher Huxley Hall

Surrounded by scenic countryside and overlooked by Beeston Castle (whose history is quite a bit shorter since it wasn't built until 1225), the Hall provides a distinguished base from which to explore this part of the county. The letting rooms here are very large, ensuite, full of character, and in addition to all the usual amenities, each is supplied with a flask containing fresh water from the Hall's own well. Guests approach their bedrooms by means of grand Elizabethan staircases: breakfast is served in a magnificent room overlooking the garden. This exceptional establishment also offers its guests the use of the Hall's private swimming pool. *Higher Huxley Hall, Huxley, Chester, CH3 9BZ. Tel: 01829 781484*

The Welsh Borders

Awake or asleep, the medieval Lords of the Marches made sure their swords were close at hand. At any time, a band of wild-haired Welshmen might rush down from the hills to attack the hated Normans who had dispossessed them of their land. A thousand years earlier their enemies had been the Romans and the centuries-old struggle would only end when one of their own people, Henry Tudor, defeated Richard III in 1485 and ascended the throne as Henry VII. Conflict was to flare up again during the Civil War when the Welsh supported the Royalist forces against mainly Parliamentary Cheshire but nowadays the valley of the Dee is both peaceful and picturesque and nowhere more so than the area around Farndon on the Denbighshire border.

Farndon Map 2 ref C6
7 miles S of Chester off the B5130

Built on a hillside overlooking the River Dee, Farndon is literally a stone's throw from Wales. Most travellers agree that the best approach to the principality is by way of this little town and its ancient bridge. Records show that building of the bridge began in 1345 and it is one of only two surviving medieval bridges in the county, the other being in Chester.

From Farndon's bridge, riverside walks by the Dee extend almost up to its partner in Chester. During the Civil War, Farndon's strategic position between Royalist North Wales and parliamentarian Cheshire led to many skirmishes here. Those stirring events are colourfully depicted in a stained glass window in the church, although only the Royalist heroes are included.

One Farndon man who deserves a memorial of some kind but doesn't have one is ***John Speed***, the famous cartographer, who was born here in 1542. He followed his father's trade as a tailor, married and had 18 children, and was nearly 50 before he was able to devote himself full time to researching and producing his beautifully drawn maps. Fortunately, he lived to the age of 87 and his fifty-four Maps of England and Wales were the first really accurate ones to be published.

The Farndon Arms Inn is a ravishing black and white building, decked in summer with huge hanging baskets of colourful flowers. Parts of this lovely building date back to the 1700s when it was a coaching inn on the old London to Anglesey route. Travellers would pause here for refreshment before their coach resumed its journey along the High Street, crossed the ancient bridge over the River Dee, and found themselves in Wales. Today, this outstanding inn is owned and run by the Bouchier family, Martin and Stephanie, along with Martin's parents, Sylvia and Keith. Martin can proudly

The Farndon Arms Inn

claim to be the fifth generation of his family to be licensees and that long tradition of hospitality is evident in the superb amenities and the exceptional quality of the food and service. Martin is the chef and his menus offer a remarkable range of old favourites and innovative newcomers: steaks of "I'll never manage this" proportions, or simple bangers and mash; an authentic black pudding, or melted goat's cheese on a bed of French leaf under a tomato fondue; Thai vegetable sizzler with coconut, or dishes featuring ostrich, kangaroo and even alligator meat. A great place to eat, but also a great place to stay. There are six comfortable, en-suite letting rooms providing a perfect base from which to explore Chester, just a few miles away, the western part of the county, and the principality of Wales. *The Farndon Arms Inn & Restaurant, High Street, Farndon, CH3 7PU. Tel: 01829 270570*

Rossett *Map 1 ref C6*

6 miles S of Chester off the A483

In Rossett, a pleasant village beside the River Alyn, and about a mile across the border into North Wales, is **The Golden Grove Inn**, a very special hostelry run by Kath Morris and her daughter Claire. Here, history strikes as an almost tangible force when you enter the inn's portals for the first time. The entrance and reception area of what is now the bar, (including a tiny snug bar) was the original 13th century Inn in its entirety. The low oak beams and ornate carved dark wood bar were additions during the 1600's. There are three dates carved into the intricate workings of the bar, but they are well hidden unless you know where to look.

The Golden Grove Inn

Naturally, such an ancient establishment has its own ghost, one James Clarke who actually expired at the inn on April 21st, 1880. James was generally believed to be the landlady's lover; certainly, she had him buried in the courtyard and erected a headstone to his memory.

Today, the Grove's restaurant is situated exactly where the courtyard used to be and James' headstone still stands in silent memorial to a man who clearly appreciated earthly pleasures. So he would surely have approved the excellent food prepared by the Golden Grove's chef, Scott Milne, with bar snacks on offer every lunchtime and evening, an à la carte menu and carvery available on Friday and Saturday evenings and Sunday lunchtimes.

The Golden Grove acquired a Civil Marriage licence in 1997 and this romantic old inn with its spacious gardens, ideal for wedding photographs, now offers complete arrangements for the ceremony and reception. There's even accommodation available in the pretty, one-bedroom cottage next door which can be rented at any time of the year, and any time now in the bed and breakfast rooms currently being planned. *The Golden Grove, Llyndir Lane, Burton Green, Rossett, Denbighshire, LL12 0AS. Tel: 01244 570445*

Higher Kinnerton
6 miles SW of Chester off the A55/A5104

Map 1 ref B5

Lying just over the Welsh border, lies one of the oldest and most picturesque coaching inns in north Wales. **The Royal Oak** boasts a resident ghost and stands where one of the most famous trees in the country once towered. Here in September 1644 King Charles I, fleeing Cromwell's troops after his defeat at Chester, evaded his pursuers by hiding amidst the branches of the Kinnerton Oak. Derek Thompson, an accomplished artist who runs the Royal Oak together with his wife Lee, has inscribed this romantic tale around the walls of the old beamed snug. It's just one of the many charming features here, along with the inglenook crackling with log fires and the fascinating collection of old pots and water jugs.

The Royal Oak

The Royal Oak is also renowned for its restaurant, a distinguished 1993 building where, it's generally agreed, you'll find the best food in the area. A team of top chefs create superb dishes using top quality ingredients such as salmon from the nearby River Dee, trout, local game and selected steak. And if you are just looking for a light meal, then the bar menu offers an excellent choice of filled baguettes or jacket potatoes, ploughman's and sandwiches. The Royal Oak is a truly exceptional hidden place, a mere six miles from the centre of Chester. *The Royal Oak, Higher Kinnerton, Flintshire, CH4 9BE. Tel: 01244 660871*

The Mount in Higher Kinnerton offers quite exceptional bed and breakfast facilities in a spacious old house, set in a lovely 3 acre garden of fine trees, mixed borders, roses and interesting shrubs. The house was built in 1860 and many of the stately old trees were also planted around that time. Garden-lovers who visit The Mount will find their hosts, Jonathan and Rachel Major, happy to talk about their own gardens (which include a large kitchen garden) and well-informed about other gardens and nurseries in the area.

The Mount Bed & Breakfast

The Mount is a restful, tranquil place, attractively decorated with such features as a wonderful old dolls' house, collections of egg shaped objets d'art and custard glasses, along with open fires and wooden floors. There are three letting rooms, two of them en suite, the third with its own private bathroom with shower: all of them enjoy superb views over the gardens. Guests are free to make use of the tennis court and croquet lawn, and dinner is available by arrangement. A non-smoking house, The Mount is well placed for exploring North Wales, Cheshire and Shropshire. *The Mount, Higher Kinnerton, Chester, CH4 9BQ. Tel: 01244 660275 Fax: 01244 660275*

Penyffordd   Map 1 ref B5
8 miles SW of Chester off the A5104

The Millstone Inn, situated in the heart of Penyffordd village, takes its name from the old barn nearby which was once a Mill. At that time, the old Chester to Denbigh railway passed close by and sidings were specially built for freight trains to collect the grain from the Mill. All that activity has gone, and the Inn itself is also quite different now. The 150-year old building still looks much the same outside, but in early 1998 the entire interior was completely refurbished. Carol and Dave Webster now preside over a smart new pub but one where the old traditions of hospitality haven't been forgotten. Carol looks after the kitchen and offers a set menu along with

The Millstone Inn

daily specials, - anything from a simple sandwich to a hearty steak. Real ales, (Greenalls & Tetleys) are always available, plus a guest beer, and The Millstone is well known for its choice of half a dozen or so lagers. An additional attraction here is the beer garden with its bowling green and children's play area. *The Millstone Inn, Hawarden Road, Penyffordd, nr Chester, CH4 0JE. Tel: 01244 550540*

Old Warren, Broughton   *Map 1 ref B5*
7 miles SW of Chester off the A55/A5104

Although only a few miles from the centre of Chester, the **Spinning Wheel Tavern and Restaurant** is very much a hidden place. To find it, take the A55 from Chester towards Holywell and Wales. When you see the sign for Broughton, follow the slip road to the island and turn left. Follow this road for about half a mile and on your right you'll see a sign for Old Warren, a No Through Road.

Turn here and, about half a mile further, you've arrived at this popular free house which local people from miles around seem to have absolutely no problem in finding. The attractive black and white building dates back to the early 1800s when it was called The Old Hawarden Castle, after the castle a couple of miles north that saw

Spinning Wheel Tavern and Restaurant

some bitter fighting during the Civil War. Inside, gleaming brass and copper everywhere attracts the eye, along with lanterns, teapots, old kettles and pans. But the main reason people return to the Spinning Wheel Tavern again and again is to sample Michael and Margaret Vernon's quite exceptional menu.

The Vernons have owned and run the tavern since 1981 and they have brought their selection of food to perfection. Whatever your preference: meat, fish, poultry or vegetarian, you'll find here a wide choice of carefully-prepared, beautifully-presented dishes. And if you just want a sandwich, that too will be freshly made. The regular specialities of the house include Steak Diane and Tournedos Rossini, but each day the blackboard lists even more options. Children have a special menu of their own: in the evening, if the child is accompanied by an adult having a meal, anything on this list is served free. The Spinning Wheel Tavern is decidedly one of those hidden places you must track down. *Spinning Wheel Tavern & Restaurant, Old Warren, Broughton, nr Chester, CH4 0EG. Tel: 01244 531068*

Saltney

Map 1 ref C5

3 miles SW of Chester off the A5104

For centuries, the ferry boat from Saltney on the south side of the River Dee provided a vital link for travellers from north Wales making their way to the great city of Chester. Modern roads put the ferrymen out of business a long time ago but their memory is honoured at **The Saltney Ferry**, run by Terry and Theresa Malone.

The Saltney Ferry

Old prints of Chester around the walls of their welcoming pub recall those bygone days. Terry is a Member of the British Institute of Innkeeping, so he knows a thing or two (or three) about providing his customers with ales served in perfect condition: John Smith's and Theakston's, along with all the usual favourites. The Saltney Ferry doesn't serve food but it does provide a variety of entertainment: karaoke on Friday nights, live music on Sunday evenings, and from time to time, themed evenings featuring the cuisine and beverages of one particular country. *The Saltney Ferry, Mainwaring Drive, Saltney, nr Chester, CH4 0AG. Tel: 01244 680063*

CHAPTER THREE
Cheshire Peaks & Plains

Gatehouse, Beeston Castle

Chapter 3 - Area Covered

*For precise location of places please refer to the colour
maps found at the rear of the book.*

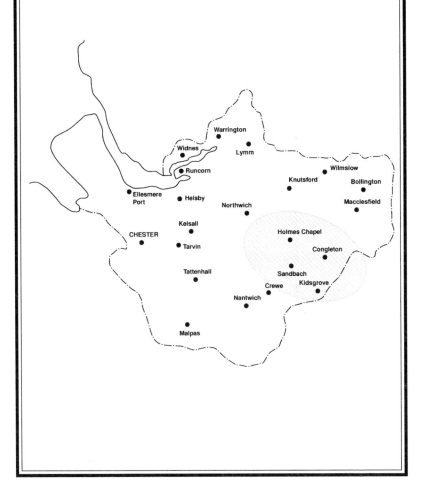

3
Cheshire Peaks & Plains

Introduction

To the east rise the Peak District hills, westwards gently undulating pastures and woods drop down to the Cheshire Plain. This is an area of sudden and striking contrasts. Within half a mile you can find yourself travelling out of lowland Cheshire into some of the highest and wildest countryside; acres of lonely uplands with rugged gritstone crags, steep valleys watered by moorland streams. Here too is the old salt town of Middlewich, and Sandbach with its famous Saxon crosses, along with a host of quiet, attractive villages. The busy M6 cuts through the area, north to south, but you have only to drive a few miles off the motorway to find yourself wandering along winding country lanes between fertile fields.

Congleton

Congleton, in the foothills of the Pennines, was an inhabited place as long ago as the Stone Age. The remains of a 5000-year-old chambered tomb known as **The Bridestones** can be seen beside the hill road running eastwards from the town to the A523 road to Leek. In Elizabethan times, the townspeople of Congleton seem to have had a passion for bear-baiting. On one occasion, when the town bear died they handed 16 shillings to the Bear Warden to acquire another beast. The money had originally been collected to buy a town bible: this disgraceful misappropriation of funds gave rise to the ditty: *"Congleton rare, Congleton rare, sold the bible to buy a bear"*. Known locally as the *"Bear Town"*, Congleton was the very last town in England to outlaw the cruel practice of bear-baiting. A more attractive distinction is the fact that it is also one the few towns in Cheshire where the medieval street pattern has remained intact and where the curfew bell is still rung each night at 8pm.

It's no surprise to find that *The Lion & Swan Hotel* is the oldest building in Congleton. Originally a 16th century coaching inn on the old Manchester to London route, this grand old building with its superb black and white half-timbered frontage has been offering travellers excellent accommodation and refreshment for centuries.

The Lion & Swan Hotel

Fully restored to its Tudor glory, the Lion & Swan has a wealth of exposed, dark oak beams and elaborately carved fireplaces, as well as the oldest window in the town, dating from 1596. Along with oak settles dating from 1676, they give a wonderful ambience to the intimate and sophisticated Candlesticks Restaurant which offers the finest of English and continental cuisine, an extensive wine list and superb service. There is a choice of two relaxing bars in which to enjoy a pre-dinner drink and all the 21 en-suite bedrooms are sumptuously decorated. The Lion & Swan also holds a licence for Civil Marriages and it's difficult to imagine a more romantic and memorable setting for a wedding and reception. *Lion & Swan Hotel, Swan Bank, Congleton, CW12 1JR. Tel: 01260 273115*

Congleton's impressive Venetian Gothic style **Town Hall**, built in 1866, contains some interesting exhibits recalling its long history. Amongst them are displays recording the work of such ancient civic officials as the swine-catcher, the chimney-looker and the ale-taster, and aids to domestic harmony like the bridle for nagging wives which used to be fastened to a wall in the market place.

Close by is Capitol Walk, Congleton's popular indoor shopping area, and here you'll find **Strawberry Fields Café**. This is the place to make for when your feet are killing you and you are more than ready for a quick pick-me-up of a wholesome, tasty snack accompanied by piping-hot tea or coffee. The Capitol Walk complex opened in 1989 and so did Cheryl German and Jackie Nutter's friendly and

Strawberry Fields Café

welcoming café. A sweeping, spiral staircase leads up to their domain with its tiled floor and umbrella-shaded tables but there is also a ramp for visitors who might find the steps difficult. The regular menu includes a hearty, but modestly-priced traditional breakfast (or an even more modestly-priced budget breakfast), a tempting choice of home baked scones, tarts, tea-cakes, pies, gingerbread and lemon meringue, toasties and well-stuffed jacket potatoes. Also, there's always a home made soup, and a good choice of freshly made sandwiches, rolls and BIG salads. Non-smokers have their own protected area. *Strawberry Fields Café, Capitol Walk, High Street, Congleton, CW12 1WB. Tel: 01260 298078*

Congleton developed as an important textile town during the 18th century with many of its mills involved in silk manufacture, cotton spinning and ribbon weaving. In **Mill Green** near the River Dane, you can still see part of the very first silk mill to operate here.

Astbury *Map 3 ref H5*
2 miles SW of Congleton on the A34

The pretty little village of Astbury, set around a triangular village green, was once more important than neighbouring Congleton which is why it has a much older church, built between 1350 and 1540. Arguably the finest parish church in the county, St Mary's is famous for its lofty recessed spire (which rises from a tower almost detached from the nave), and the superb timber work inside: a richly carved ceiling, intricate tracery on the rood screen, and a lovely Jacobean font cover. But just three miles down the A34 is an even more remarkable building.

Black and white half-timbered houses have almost become a symbol for the county of Cheshire and the most stunning example is undoubtedly **Little Moreton Hall** (National Trust), a *"wibbly wobbly"* house which provided a memorable location for Granada TV's adaptation of *"Moll Flanders"*. The only bricks to be seen are in the chimneys, and The Hall's huge overhanging gables, slanting walls, and great stretches of leaded windows, create wonderfully complex patterns, all magically reflected in the still flooded moat. Ralph Moreton began construction in 1480 and the fabric of this magnifi-

Little Moreton Hall

cent house has changed little since the 16th century. A richly panelled Great Hall, parlour and chapel show off superb Elizabethan
plaster and wood work. Free guided tours give visitors a fascinating
insight into Tudor life, and there's also a beautifully reconstructed
Elizabethan knot garden with clipped box hedges and a period herb
garden.

Directly across the road from Little Moreton Hall is *Cuttleford
Farm*, parts of which are almost as old, dating back to the 16th
century. This attractive old house, built in warm red brick and surrounded by the open fields of the 160-acre mixed farm, makes an
ideal bed and breakfast base for exploring this part of the county.

Cuttleford Farm

The Peak District National Park, too, is just a few miles to the east.
Carol and Geoffrey Downs have lived here for 38 years and have
been offering bed & breakfast for the past 16 years, so they know
exactly how to make their guests welcome and comfortable.
Cuttleford Farm has three inviting rooms to let: a double en-suite
on one side of the house, and a double and a twin with a shared
bathroom on the other. Evening meals are not provided, (there are
many good local eating establishments), but guests will find a substantial breakfast and if they wish, a packed lunch. An additional
attraction is the outdoor tennis court. Children are welcome, but
the house is not suitable for the disabled. *Cuttleford Farm, Astbury,
Congleton, CW12 4SD. Tel: 01260 272499*

About a mile south of Cuttleford Farm is the *Rode Hall Estate*.
It was an 18th century owner of the estate, Randle Wilbraham,
who built the famous folly of *Mow Cop* (National Trust) to enhance

Saxon Crosses, Sandbach

Mow Cop, Nr Astbury

the view from his mansion. This mock ruin stands atop a rocky hill 1100 ft above sea level, just yards from the Staffordshire border. On a clear day, the views are fantastic: Alderley Edge to the north, the Pennines to the north-east, south to Cannock Chase and Shropshire, and westwards across Cheshire.

Sandbach   Map 3 ref G6
1 mile SW of Junction 17 of the M6
Sandbach's former importance as a stopping place for coaches (both stage and motor) is evident in the attractive old half-timbered inns and houses, some of them thatched, which line the main street.

Sandbach's handsome market square is dominated by its two famous stone crosses, 16 and 11 feet tall. These superbly carved crosses (actually only the shafts have survived) were created some time in the 9th century, and the striking scenes are believed to represent the conversion of Mercia to Christianity during the reign of King Penda. A plaque at their base notes that they were restored in 1816 *"after destruction by iconoclasts"* - i.e. the Puritans. The restorers had to recover fragments from here and there: some had been used as street paving, cottage steps or in the walls of a well. Somehow they fitted the broken stones together, like pieces of a jigsaw, and the result is immensely impressive.

Lovers of beautiful old things should make a bee-line for Sandbach and **Saxon Cross Antiques**, run by John and Christine Jones in two separate premises. In Bold Street they have taken over an imposing century-old building, formerly the central offices of the Co-operative Society, and filled it with an amazing range of antiques from every age, of every size and description. Their second show-room is housed in the former Hope Street School and the early 18th century barn at its rear. In this splendid setting, with its roof beams of old ship's timbers, they specialise in antique furniture of every kind, some of it dating back to Tudor times. John has been fascinated by antiques ever since, as a boy of 12, he began restoring tin

Saxon Cross Antiques

plate toys and he is happy to share his wealth of knowledge with his customers. Due for completion by early 1999 is John and Christine's ambitious project to create a "Children's Transport Museum" at their Hope Street premises. It will be the largest of its kind in Britain, possibly in Europe, and they already have a huge number of exhibits ranging from hobby horses to pedal cars. Entry will be free, with a donation box for the benefit of charities. *Saxon Cross Antiques, 1, Bold Street, Sandbach, CW11 1GR. Tel: 01270 753005 / 753009*

Arclid   *Map 3 ref H5*
2 miles NE of Sandbach at the crossroads of the A50 and A534
The tiny village of Arclid, nevertheless, boasts its own hospital and a friendly village pub. The first recorded licensee of **The Rose & Crown** was Thomas Yates, back in 1850. Like many landlords at that time, Thomas ran the pub as a sideline: his main occupation was as a joiner and builder. Today's licensees, Kev and Sue Moores,

The Rose & Crown

take the job rather more seriously and have made The Rose & Crown a popular centre with an excellent reputation for its well-prepared food (by Sue) and its well-kept Burtonwood ales (by Kev). Meals are served every lunchtime and evening, (all day at weekends), and include a good selection of meat, fish and vegetarian dishes, snacks, salads and sandwiches, daily specials and children's basket meals.

There's good access for the disabled and, for warm days, a patio area at the rear with a small aviary. Entertainments include occasional karaoke and folk-song evenings, and, a special attraction, a steam rally held here in early April. The pub also offers visitors a beer garden and a play area for children. The Rose & Crown can be found just a mile from junction 17 of the M6, at the crossroads of the A50 and A534. *The Rose & Crown, Newcastle Road, Arclid, nr Sandbach, CW11 9SM. Tel: 01477 500543*

Holmes Chapel   Map 3 ref G5
4 miles N of Sandbach on the A50/A54

In the mid-18th century, the little village of Holmes Chapel was stirred by two important events. In 1738, John Wesley came and preached outside St Luke's Church. Fifteen years later, on July 10th, 1753, a disastrous fire swept through the village. When the flames were finally quenched, only two buildings had survived the blaze: St Luke's Church and **The Old Red Lion** alongside.

This charming old hostelry with its exposed beams, wood panelling and open fire, was then an important coaching inn and its old stables are still standing at the rear of the house. Nowadays, the

The Old Red Lion

Old Red Lion is part of the Allied Domecq Leisure group and run by Phil and Carol Crowther. Phil is well known for his culinary skills so he is in charge of the food, offering a regular menu of home made soup, hearty main meals such as gammon steak, vegetarian choices, and traditional treats such as spotted dick. Along with daily blackboard specials, the menu is available at lunchtimes (noon - 2pm) and evenings (6pm - 8.30pm) every day, except on Sunday evening. The Crowthers lay on a quiz night on Thursdays, and sun worshippers will be pleased to know that The Old Red Lion's patio and beer garden is a positive sun trap. *The Old Red Lion, 17, London Road, Holmes Chapel, CW4 7AQ. Tel: 01477 532296*

Middlewich
Map 3 ref G5

5 miles NW of Sandbach on the A54

The Romans called their settlement here *Salinae*, meaning saltworks. Excavations have revealed outlines of their long, narrow, timber workshops, brine pits and even a jar with the word *"AMYRCA"* scratched on it. (Amurca was the Latin name for brine waste and was used throughout the Empire as a cleansing agent). In modern times, it was the need for Cheshire's salt manufacturers to get their cumbersome product to markets in the Midlands and the south which gave a great impetus to the building of canals in the county. Middlewich was particularly well-provided for with its own **Middlewich Branch Canal** linking the town to both the **Shropshire Union** and the **Trent & Mersey** canals.

Located alongside the Trent and Mersey canal is **The Newton Brewery Inn**, a very popular stopping place for canal travellers who make good use of the inn's moorings and its large, attractive garden set beside the towpath. The scene is particularly busy here in mid-June when the popular Middlewich Folk and Boat Festival takes place.

The Newton Brewery Inn

Dating back to the 1830's, the inn takes its name from the brewery that preceded it on this site and, appropriately enough, nowadays it specialises in offering excellent Marston and other ales plus, in summer, a Bavarian lager called *"Summer Wheat Beer"*. The Newton Brewery is very much a family affair, run by Merle and Phil Flaherty together with their sons Ken and Biff, and daughter Laura. They enjoy setting up special events, so there's a quiz on Tuesday evenings, karaoke on Friday and Saturday evenings, and afternoon games on Sundays. The inn is open from noon onwards, every day, except during the winter when it opens at 2pm on Monday, Tuesday and Wednesday. *The Newton Brewery Inn, 68, Webbs Lane, Middlewich, CW10 9DN. Tel: 01606 833502*

During the Civil War, Middlewich witnessed two of the bloodiest battles fought in the county. In March 1644, Royalists trapped Cromwell's men in the narrow lanes and alleys of the town and slaughtered 200 of them. A few managed to find refuge in **St Michael's Church** which has changed greatly since those days but has some notable old carvings and a curiosity in the form of a carved coat of arms of the Kinderton family of nearby Kinderton Hall. Their crest shows a dragon eating a child, a reference to the occasion on which Baron Kinderton killed a local dragon as it was devouring a child. The incident apparently took place at Moston, near Sandbach, and a lane there is still called Dragon Lane.

The Vaults started life as a private Brewing House several hundred years ago before the present pub was established earlier this century - although that's quite long enough to establish a sound tradition of hospitality, a tradition that the Flaherty family, - Allan and Jean, together with their son Matthew - keep very much alive.

The Vaults

Their lively and popular pub specialises in fine ales, with Tetleys beers always available and traditional guest ales on tap during the summer. Before becoming a licensee, Allan was a drayman for some 15 years, so you can be pretty confident he'll make sure that any pint he draws is a good one. The atmosphere is always welcoming, but towards the end of the week it becomes even more so with a succession of entertainments: a disco on Thursday and Friday, a karaoke on Saturday, and on Sunday a 70s and 80s disco. They're all free and all start around 8pm. Children are welcome and for fine, warm days there's a pleasant beer garden at the back of the pub where you can also savour a well-kept pint. *The Vaults, Wheelock Street,Middlewich, Cheshire CW10 9AG Tel: 01606 832229*

Church Minshull　　　　　　　　　　　　*Map 2 ref F6*
5 miles SW of Middlewich on minor road off the A530

This picturesque little village is known to a few people as the home of Elizabeth Minshull before she became the third wife of the poet

John Milton in 1660. Many, many more know it as a place to find excellent food and real ales. You really should not miss **The Badger Inn**, designated as a Building of Historic and Architectural Interest and attractively located close to the River Weaver. Built in 1760, the inn was originally known as the Brookes Arms, named after the family who were great landowners in the Mere and Tatton area. In a play of words on their name, the Brookes coat of arms bears two brocks, the old English name for badgers, (brocks/Brookes), and so led to the inn's present name.

The Badger Inn

The Badger's riverside location makes it popular with walkers and boating enthusiasts, particularly in the summer when the lovely beer garden, conservatory and children's play area come into their own. It's an ideal family pub in that sense, and also because it's run by a friendly and welcoming family, Richard and Ann Kay together with their son, Patrick. The menu here is a distinguished one, offering traditional dishes, home made pastas, vegetarian options, chimmichangas (flour tortillas with cream topped with salsa and cheese), as well as filled baguettes, sandwiches, children's meals and, on weekdays, a Senior Citizen Special at lunchtime. The warm and relaxed atmosphere of the Inn is enhanced by the old brickwork and cosy alcoves and, of course, there are badgers in some form or another wherever you look! *The Badger Inn, Nantwich Road, Church Minshull, CW5 6DY. Tel: 01270 522607*

Wettenhall

Map 2 ref F6

7 miles SW of Middlewich on minor road off the B5074

Wettenhall is a pretty little village surrounded by open country-side, and records show that it has enjoyed the amenity of a public house since 1651. The hostelry used to be called The Little John and was located on the very spot where *The Little Man Inn* now stands. The change of name came about in the 19th century when local licensees decided to pay tribute to a real life "little man". Sammy Grice, less than four feet tall, was much valued for his skill in pro-

The Little Man Inn

viding vent pegs for them, and skewers for the butchers of Chester. Today, Harry Goodwin and Rosemary Turner run this inviting village pub which offers an extensive choice of good wholesome food, ranging from the hearty (braised steak in ale, for example), through the vegetarian (wheat & walnut casserole, perhaps), to simple snacks, basket meals and sandwiches. Their welcoming establishment is attractively decorated with lots of fine china plates, brass hunting horns, local pictures, and, as a rather unusual feature, some of the bar stools are actually old milk churns made comfortable with cushions, or in one case, with a genuine saddle. *The Little Man Inn, Winsford Rd., Wettenhall, nr Winsford, CW7 4DL. Tel: 01270 528203*

Tarporley

Map 2 ref E5

9 miles W of Chester on the A51/A49

In the days when most of this area was part of **Delamere Forest**, Tarporley was the headquarters of the verderers or forest wardens. It was from Tarporley in the early 17th century that John Done, Chief Forester and Hereditary Bow-bearer of Delamere entertained King James to a hunt. The chase was, he reported, a great success: *"deer, both red and fallow, fish and fowl, abounded in the meres".* A gratified King rewarded his host with a knighthood. At that time, the verderers had their own courts in which they meted out rough justice to offenders against the forest laws.

One such court was at **Utkinton**, just north of the town, and in an old farmhouse there stands a column formed by an ancient forest tree, its roots still in the ground. When the court was in session, the wardens would place on this tree the symbol of their authority, the Hunting Horn of Delamere. The farmhouse is not open to the public but the horn, dating from around 1120, has survived and can be seen at the **Grosvenor Museum** in Chester. Another impressive survivor is the Tarporley Hunt Club which is primarily a dining club for hunting people and still has an annual banquet in the town. Founded in 1762, it is now the oldest Hunt Club in the country.

Enjoying a prominent position on the High Street, is the 200-year-old **Foresters Arms**, run by Stuart Hulse and Lesley Rowland. They took over in 1993 and, with great care, have refurbished the whole pub while retaining its charming old features. Their upgrading of this picturesque hostelry, which was formerly a coaching inn

The Foresters Arms

with extensive stables, earned them a Two Crown rating from the English Tourist Board. They were also awarded an additional accolade for the quality of the accommodation in the three double bedrooms, - each room furnished in a slightly different way to reflect the individual character of the pub itself. The food, served every lunchtime and evening except Sunday evening, is quite outstanding, a well-thought out selection of tasty starters, (Chinese spring rolls, for example), hearty main courses, fish and vegetarian dishes, as well as a good choice of sandwiches and snacks. Other attractions include a pleasant patio area to the rear, a separate games room, live music on Friday nights and, on Sunday nights, a quiz open to all. *The Foresters Arms, 92, High Street, Tarporley, CW6 0AX. Tel: 01829 733151*

Willington
Map 2 ref E5

3 miles N on minor road from centre of Tarporley

A very good reason for seeking out the village of Willington near Kelsall, is to pay a visit to **The Boot Inn**, a real hidden gem of a traditional English country pub. Originally a beerhouse situated within a row of cottages built in warm red brick and sandstone, it now occupies the whole row and is a captivating olde worlde pub with great character, style and charm. There are quarry-tiled floors, open fires, old beams, a large penny-farthing bicycle assembled from old penny and threepenny pieces and some fascinating memorabilia on display - find out why the pub is known to its long standing regulars as *"The Cat"*.

The Boot Inn

Mike and Liz offer guests a warm welcome, along with a choice of different ales including guest ales from around the country. Their charming restaurant serves quality fresh food from a menu which includes popular favourites such as home-made soup and steak and kidney pie, along with some tempting alternatives, a good choice of vegetarian dishes and daily lunchtime and evening specials (such as chateaubriand or smoked haddock with a rarebit topping served on a tomato and chive sauce). In fine weather, take a seat on the patio or in the garden and, if you enjoy walking, The Boot is an excellent base. Explore the picturesque local area known as Little Switzerland or take a longer walk to Primrose Wood. You can even pick up a copy of The Boot's own leaflet of walks. *The Boot Inn, Boothsdale, Willington, nr Tarporley, CW6 0NH. Tel: 01829 - 751375*

Little Budworth   *Map 2 ref E5*
4 miles NE of Tarporley on minor road off the A49 or A54

A few miles east of Willington is **Little Budworth Common Country Park**, a pleasant area of heathland and woods ideal for picnics and walking. The nearby village enjoys splendid views over Budworth Pool but will be better known to motor racing enthusiasts for the **Oulton Park** racing circuit a mile or so to the south.

The Red Lion Hotel in Little Budworth was built some two hundred years ago as a coaching inn and the original mounting steps still stand at the front of the building. Inside, the open fires, traditional furnishings and gleaming collection of brass and copper lamps, kettles, pots and pans, create an immediately inviting atmosphere. Pauline and Alan Burgess came here in 1996 and very quickly established a reputation for providing good food (cooked by Pauline) and a warm, hospitable welcome (from both!). The set menu changes

The Red Lion Hotel

from time to time but will typically include dishes such as honeyed Lamb Chops or home made salmon pie. Food is served at lunchtimes and evenings during the week, from noon until 9pm on Sundays. *The Red Lion Hotel, Vicarage Lane, Little Budworth, nr Tarporley, CW6 9BY. Tel: 01829 760275*

Tiverton
Map 2 ref E6

2 miles S of Tarporley on the A49

Set around a delightful village green, Tiverton lies almost in the shadow of **Beeston Castle**, with the **Shropshire Union Canal** running nearby. Enjoying an excellent position alongside the bank of the canal, **The Shady Oak** is another hidden gem well worth seeking out. Its canalside location, beside Bate's Mill Bridge, makes it very popular with boating people, towpath walkers and, indeed, with any one lucky enough to know about it.

The Shady Oak

The building itself dates back to the early 1800's and has preserved many attractive features such as the old nut & bolt style beams. Andy and Gill Holden are its popular hosts, offering guests a choice selection of food and ale, all day, every day. The comprehensive menu includes a tempting variety of main meals and snacks, vegetarians will find themselves well-catered for, and there's a beautifully maintained beer garden where you can enjoy your food and drink on fairweather days. Should you fancy a little sight-seeing, the twin castles of Beeston (English Heritage) and Peckforton (privately-owned, but open to the public) are only a couple of miles away. *The Shady Oak, 8 Batesmill Lane, Tiverton, nr Tarporley, CW6 9UE. Tel: 01829 733159*

About half a mile north of Tiverton, at the junction of the A49 and the A51, stands **The Red Fox**, built as a farmhouse in the 1700s and with a warm, welcoming atmosphere that recalls the great tradition of farmhouse hospitality.

The Red Fox

The inn's popular landlords, Patricia and Henry Cunningham, have many years experience in the catering trade and the excellent food they serve here (twice daily, every day) has made The Red Fox one of the most popular eating places in the area. Their extensive menu, changed every six months or so, offers a wide choice of starters, grills, and "hot 'n' spicy" dishes, along with pasta, fish and vegetarian options. Those with smaller appetites will appreciate the selection of hot and cold platters, or sandwiches, and children have their own menu. The range of choice is made even wider by the daily specials.

You can enjoy your meal anywhere in the inn itself, or in the adjoining conservatory which is a non-smoking area. The Red Fox is the kind of hostelry where you might well want to linger, even overnight. If so, the Cunninghams have two letting rooms, a double and a single, available all year round. *The Red Fox, Four Lanes End, Tiverton, nr Tarporley, CW6 9LZ. Tel: 01829 733152*

Beeston

Map 2 ref E6

3 miles SW of Tarporley on minor road off the A49

A craggy cliff suddenly rising 500ft from the Cheshire Plain, its summit crowned by the ruins of **Beeston Castle** (English Heritage), Beeston Hill is one of the most dramatic sights in the county. Built around 1220, the castle didn't see any military action until the Civil War. On one rather ignominious occasion during that conflict, a Royalist captain and just eight musketeers managed to capture the mighty fortress and its garrison of 60 soldiers without firing a shot. A few years later, Cromwell ordered that the castle be *"slighted"*, or partially destroyed, but this *"Castle in the Air"* is still very imposing with walls 30ft high and a well 366ft deep. An old legend asserts that Richard II tipped a hoard of coins, gold and jewels down the well, but no treasure has yet been discovered.

Gatehouse, Beeston Castle

The castle hill is a popular place for picnics, and it's worth climbing it just to enjoy the spectacular views which extend across seven counties and over to a *"twin"* castle. **Peckforton Castle** looks just as medieval as Beeston but was, in fact, built in 1844 for the first Lord Tollemache who spared no expense in re-creating features such as a vast Great Hall and a keep with towers 60ft tall. The architect Gilbert Scott later praised Peckforton as *"the very height of masquerading"*. Its authentic medieval appearance has made the castle a favourite location for film and television companies, and on Sundays and Bank Holidays during the season the Middle Ages are brought to life here with mock battles and tournaments. The castle also offers guided tours, refreshments and a speciality shop.

Cholmondeley Castle   Map 2 ref E7
7 miles S of Tarporley off the A49

If you continue south from Beeston on the A49, after about six miles you will reach **Cholmondeley Castle** and its famous gardens. They were first laid out in the early years of the 19th century shortly after the Castle was built. The Castle itself, a marvellous mock-medieval construction, is not open to the public, but visitors are welcome to explore the 30 acre garden which includes a water garden and woodland walks. There are plants for sale, a lakeside picnic area, a gift shop and tea room.

CHAPTER FOUR
The Vale Royal

Anderton Boat Lift

Chapter 4 - Area Covered

For precise location of places please refer to the colour maps found at the rear of the book.

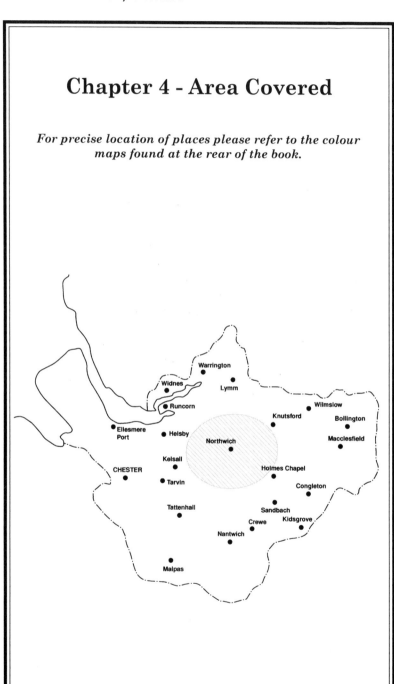

4
The Vale Royal

Introduction

The Vale Royal, - an attractive name for a very attractive part of the county. It was Prince Edward, later Edward I, who named it so and it was he who founded the great Abbey of Vale Royal in fulfilment of a solemn vow made in dramatic circumstances. He was returning from the Crusades when his ship was struck by a violent storm. The Prince made a pledge to the Virgin that if his life were spared he would found an Abbey for one hundred monks. Lo!, the ship was tossed ashore, the Prince and his companions waded through the surf to safety.

In 1277, Edward, now King and with his young wife Eleanor of Castile by his side, honoured his vow by placing the first stone of *Vale Royal Abbey*. *"No monastery"* he decreed *"shall be more royal than this one in liberties, wealth and honour, throughout the whole world"*. Vale Royal Abbey indeed became the largest and most powerful Cistercian Abbey in England, a building reputedly even more glorious than Tintern or Fountains. Unlike those Abbeys, however, barely a stone of Vale Royal now remains in place. The abuse by the medieval Abbots of their vast wealth, and of their unfettered power of life and death over the inhabitants of the Vale, may partly explain why their magnificent building was so quickly and completely destroyed after Henry VIII's closure of the monasteries. Over the centuries, the county has lost many fine buildings unnecessarily but the deliberate destruction of Vale Royal Abbey must take prime place in the litany of crimes against sublime architecture.

Northwich

The Vale Royal is now a district borough centred on the old salt town of Northwich. Even before the Romans arrived, Cheshire salt was well known and highly valued. But production on a major scale at Northwich began in 1670 when rock salt was discovered in nearby Marston.

Salt may seem an inoffensive sort of product, but its extraction from the Keuper marl of the Cheshire Plain has had some quite spectacular side-effects. In Elizabethan times, John Leland, recorded that a hill at Combermere suddenly disappeared into underground workings, and Northwich later became notorious for the number of its buildings leaning at crazy angles because of subsidence. Even today, the **White Lion Inn** in Witton Street lies a complete storey lower than its original height.

The arrival in the 19th century of new processes of extraction brought different problems. In 1873, John Brunner and Ludwig Mond set up their salt works at Winnington on the northern edge of the town to manufacture alkali products based on brine. The ammonia process involved cast an appalling stench over the town and devastated vegetation for miles around. On the other hand, Brunner and Mond were model employers. They paid their work-force well, built houses for them and were amongst the first firms in the country to give their employees annual holidays with pay.

The long involvement of Northwich and Cheshire with salt production is vividly recorded at the **Salt Museum**, the only one of its kind in Britain. It stands in London Road and occupies what used to be the **Northwich Workhouse** which, like so many of those dreaded institutions, is an exceptionally handsome late-Georgian building, designed by George Latham, the architect of Arley Hall. With its

Salt Museum, Northwich

unique collection of traditional working tools, and lively displays which include working models and videos, the Salt Museum recounts the fascinating story of the county's oldest industry. Not only can ancient remains such as Roman evaporating pans and medieval salt rakes be seen, but there is also much to remind visitors of the vital part that salt plays in the modern chemical industry.

Salt plays quite a different role at ***The Seafarer Restaurant*** in Chesterway. For over a quarter of a century, the restaurant has been providing its customers with excellent food, - especially fish and chips. These have earned The Seafarer a place in The National Gourmets Guide to Fish & Chips. Owner Neil Stevenson takes great pride in only offering the finest quality freshly prepared products, served by pleasant, helpful staff in traditional seafaring surroundings. The celebrated fish dishes tend to get all the glory, but tasty chicken, meat, and vegetarian meals are also served, and children have their own, unusually extensive, menu.

The Seafarer Restaurant

The restaurant is licensed for beer and wine, and there are both smoking and non-smoking areas. The Seafarer is open every day from 11am until 10pm, but its takeaway service stays open until 11pm, serving the same top-quality food available in the restaurant itself. This is almost certainly the best fish and chip shop in Cheshire, if not in the whole of the country, - you really shouldn't miss it!. *The Seafarer Restaurant, 7, Chesterway, Northwich, CW9 5AS. Tel: 01606 43169*

Just five minutes walk from the centre of Northwich, **The Bowling Green** is one of those lovely old black and white buildings so typical of the county. It appears even more appealing in summer when the colourful window-boxes and hanging baskets are in full bloom. This ancient hostelry dates back to 1650 and the interior is much more spacious than you would imagine from outside. Here you'll find a wealth of eye-catching features, - old beams, floors of wood or quarry tiles, and lots of interesting bygones strewn around the rooms.

The Bowling Green

The regular "Ale & Hearty" menu, offering a wide choice of traditional pub food supplemented by up to half a dozen daily specials, can be thoroughly recommended. Malcolm and Susan Pye have run this popular pub since 1996 and find that one of their busiest nights is Tuesday - Quiz Night. The pub, incidentally, takes its name from the bowling green which, until about 17 years ago, lay right alongside it and is now an attractive children's play area. *The Bowling Green, 164, London Road, Leftwich, Northwich, CW9 8AA. Tel: 01606 42333*

Anderton   Map 2 ref F4
1 miles NW of Northwich on minor road off the A533
One of the most stupendous engineering feats of the canal age was the **Anderton Boat Lift**, built in 1875 and recently restored. This extraordinary construction was designed to transfer boats from the **Trent & Mersey Canal** to the **Weaver Navigation** 50ft below. Two barges would enter the upper tank, two the lower, and by pumping water out of the lower tank, the boats would exchange places. Thousands of visitors come every year to marvel at this impressive

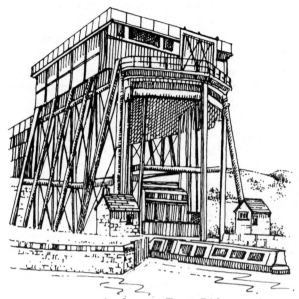

Anderton Boat Lift

structure which was conceived and designed by Edward Leader Williams who later went on to engineer the Manchester Ship Canal.

Boats - and people messing about in boats, has an endless fascination for many of us. *The Moorings Restaurant* in the Anderton Marina on the *Trent & Mersey Canal* provides a wonderful grandstand view of canal life: all those sleek river-cruisers and gaudily-decorated narrow-boats; all those proud owners polishing and scouring their craft. Jackie and James, along with Jackie's mum and dad, Dorothy and Brian, arrived at The Moorings in 1997 and

The Moorings Restaurant

have made their waterside restaurant one of the most popular stopping-places along the canal.

James perfected his culinary skills in the kitchens of London's Dorchester Hotel and he brings a metropolitan flair to a versatile menu designed to appeal to most tastes - anything from Beef Wellington through to a comprehensive vegetarian menu and "After this, I'm on a diet" desserts. The Moorings Restaurant's opening hours are11:00 am to 9:00 pm every day except Tuesdays in summer and Mondays and Tuesdays in winter. *The Moorings Restaurant, Anderton Marina, Anderton, Northwich, CW9 6AQ. Tel: 01606 - 79789*

What began as a hobby for Dave Wilson some eleven years ago has grown into the flourishing business of **Dave's Woodcrafts**. Back then, Dave was a butcher but his new career took off when he made four window boxes and two small barrows for his parents. They were so well-made that friends and neighbours asked him to make various ous pieces for them and within a few months he had abandoned butchery and set up his own woodcraft business. Today, his thriving centre provides visitors with a fascinating display of handcrafted household or garden furniture and stoneware with more than 2,000 products to choose from: rustic garden seats, troughs and tubs, bird-tables, pergolas

Dave's Woodcrafts

and arches, even bridges. And that's only part of what's on offer here. You'll also find a comprehensive range of plants and hanging baskets, fencing, flags and paving stones, a Pets' Corner and a huge stock of every kind of treat or necessity your pet might demand of you. This is a place really worth visiting and, conveniently, it's open every day from 9am until 6pm. *Dave's Woodcrafts, Daisy Bank Lane, off Soot Hill, Anderton, Northwich. Tel: 01606 784270*

About a mile north of Anderton, **Marbury Country Park** was formerly part of a large country estate, but the area is now managed by Cheshire County Council whose wardens have created a variety of habitats for plants, trees and animals. The Park lies at the edge of **Budworth Mere** and there are attractive walks and bridleways around the site where you'll also find an arboretum, picnic area and garden centre.

Broken Cross   *Map 2 ref F4*
2 miles E of Northwich on B5082

A few miles south of the Anderton Lift, **The Old Broken Cross** enjoys a lovely position beside the canal with a garden from which visitors can watch people having fun *"simply messing about in boats"*. This attractive old pub was built in the mid-1750s, originally to provide basic food and housing for the navvies, or navigators, building

The Old Broken Cross

this stretch of the **Trent & Mersey Canal**. The pub still has a relaxing, olde worlde atmosphere, with Yorkshire flag floors, old kitchen range and real fires, but the standard of the food served here nowadays has come a long way since then. Colin and Zosia McPherson offer an excellent menu, supplemented by blackboard specials and available at lunchtime (noon-2.30pm) and in the evening (5.00-9pm) every day, and all day at weekends. The first class ales include Greenalls Bitter and Mild, Caffrey's and guest ales. *The Old Broken Cross, Broken Cross Place, Rudheath, Northwich, CW9 7EB. Tel: 01606 40431*

Comberbach   *Map 2 ref F3*
3 miles NW of Northwich on minor road off the A533.

Standing in the heart of the picturesque village of Comberbach, **The Drum and Monkey** dates back to the early 1800s when it was known as *"The Avenue"*. The pub acquired its more interesting name later

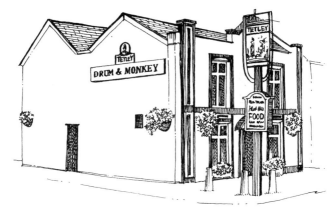

The Drum and Monkey

that century in recognition of a colourful old organ grinder who came here at weekends for many years to entertain the pub's clientele. It is a traditional village pub with excellent, well-kept ales and good, home-cooked "pub grub" at lunchtimes. Notionally, the kitchen closes at 2pm but the rules are very flexible. Should you arrive hungry a bit later, they'll find something for you even if it's just a sandwich.

Tony and Doreen Sherlock have created a wonderfully friendly atmosphere here in which locals and visitors mix freely, joining in the regular quiz nights and supporting the Sherlocks' work for local charities. At the Drum and Monkey you will find all that is best in the great tradition of the British pub very much alive and well. *The Drum and Monkey, The Avenue, Comberbach, Northwich, CW9 6HT. Tel: 01606 891417*

Arley   Map 2 ref F3
6 miles N of Northwich on a minor road off the A559

There are many grand houses in Cheshire, and many fine gardens, but at **Arley Hall and Gardens** you will find one of the grandest houses and one of the finest gardens in perfect harmony. The present Hall was completed in 1845, a few years after Rowland Egerton-Warburton arrived at Arley with his new bride, Mary Brooke. The newly-married couple took possession of a dilapidated old mansion, infested with rats and with antiquated drains from which an unbearable stench drifted through the house. Understandably, Rowland and Mary soon demolished the old hall and in its place rose a sumptuous early-Victorian stately home complete with (bearing in mind those drains) such state-of-the-art innovations as Howden's Patent Atmospheric Air Dispensers.

Arley Hall and Gardens

Rowland and Mary were both ardent gardeners and it was they who master-minded the magnificent panoramas of today's Arley Gardens. Rowland is credited with creating what is believed to be the first herbaceous border in England; his descendant, the present Viscount Ashbrook, has continued that tradition by cultivating "The Grove", an informal woodland garden planted with spring bulbs, flowering shrubs and exotic trees, a pleasing contrast to the more formal design of the main gardens. *Arley Hall & Gardens, nr Northwich, CW9 6NA. Tel: 01565 777353*

Antrobus
Map 2 ref F3

5 miles N of Northwich on minor road off the A559

Just a couple of miles from the magnificent Arley Hall and its world-famous gardens, is the pleasing little village of Antrobus, the only place in Britain to bear this name. Even the Oxford Dictionary of English Place Names is baffled by Antrobus: *"Unexplained"* it says curtly, adding as its excuse, *"Hardly English"*.

But what could be more English than **The Antrobus Arms**? Set in one and a half acres of land and surrounded by scenic country-side, this impressive building was first licensed in 1760 and ever since has been providing good food and fine ales for both locals and for travellers along the main A559 between Warrington and Northwich. Ian and Pat Littler took over here in 1997 and quickly created a very hospitable atmosphere - particularly evident on Tues-day nights when there's a sing-along around the piano. The Antrobus Arms is open every lunchtime and evening with wholesome "pub grub" available Wednesday to Sunday, and on Bank Holiday Mon-

The Antrobus Arms

days. This very customer-friendly pub also has a play area for children, and wheelchair users will find that access is easy. *The Antrobus Arms, Warrington Road, Antrobus, nr Northwich, CW9 6JD. Tel: 01606 891333*

Great Budworth

Map 2 ref F3

3 miles N of Northwich off the A559

A charming small village nowadays, *"Great"* Budworth was accorded that designation at a time when it was the largest ecclesiastical parish in all Cheshire, the administrative centre for some 35 individual communities. The imposing church on the hill, built in the 14th and 15th centuries, reflects its importance during those years. *St Mary & All Saints* attracts many visitors to its host of quaint carvings and odd faces that peer out at unexpected corners: some with staring eyes, others with their tongues poking out. There's a man near the pulpit who appears to be drowsing through some interminable sermon. Under the roof of the nave you'll find a man with a serpent, another in mid-somersault, and a minstrel playing bagpipes. The distinguished 17th century historian, Sir Peter Leycester, is buried in the Lady Chapel, and in the Warburton Chapel there is a finely carved Tudor ceiling and 13th century oak stalls - the oldest in Cheshire.

During the 19th century, Great Budworth was part of the Arley Hall estate and it is largely due to the energetic Squire Egerton-

Warburton, a *"conservationist"* well ahead of his time, that so many of the attractive old cottages in the village are still in place.

It always inspires confidence to learn that a pub has been run by the same family for many years. **The George and Dragon** in this picturesque village has been in the capable hands of the Curtin family for more than 35 years: the present generation, Malcolm and Rose have presided over this historic inn since 1982. Originally built in 1722, when the consumption of a couple of bottles of port wine over the course of an evening was considered a modest sup for any sociable person, the George and Dragon rather surprisingly greets customers with a warning against intemperate drinking. An ancient inscription in the front porch advises:

> *"As St George in armed array*
> *Doth the fiery dragon slay*
> *So mayst thou with might no less*
> *Slay that dragon drunkenness".*

So don't linger in the porch. Step inside the George and Dragon and you will find yourself enjoying a really friendly hostelry offering an excellent choice of well-prepared food and well-kept ales. The CAMRA good beer guide has been recommending the inn for the

The George & Dragon

last ten years: the Egon Ronay Pub Guide and the Good Pub Guide currently add their own plaudits. *The George & Dragon, High Street, Great Budworth, nr Northwich, CW9 6HF. Tel: 01606 891317*

Marston *Map 2 ref F4*

1 mile NE of Northwich on a minor road

In Victorian times, the **Old Salt Mine** at Marston was a huge tourist attraction. About 360 ft deep and covering 35 acres, it even brought the Tsar of Russia here in 1844. Ten thousand lamps illuminated the huge cavern as the Emperor sat down to dinner here with eminent members of the Royal Society. By the end of the century, however, subsidence caused by the mine had made some 40 houses in the village uninhabitable, and one day in 1933 a hole 50ft wide and 300ft deep suddenly appeared close to the **Trent & Mersey Canal**. Happily, the village has now stabilised itself, and at the **Lion Salt Works Museum** on most afternoons you will find volunteer workers keeping alive the only surviving open pan saltworks in Britain.

Opposite the Lion Salt Works Museum is **The Salt Barge**. It stands beside bridge 193 over the **Trent & Mersey canal**, a popular place of resort for canal travellers. The inn is much larger than it looks from outside, offering visitors no few than eight different areas in which to drink and dine, as well as an indoor children's play area complete with toys, TV and videos. Old beams and much memorabilia of canal life add to the charm of this century-old pub

The Salt Barge

which is owned and run by Lyn Brooks and Gerry Cartwright. The Salt Barge has always been well-known for its choice of fine ales, but it now offers up to 17 different brews, of which four or five change regularly. The menu is equally extensive, supplemented by a further choice of daily specials. There's live entertainment twice a month, a weekly quiz on Thursday evenings and an occasional Irish night. This lively, friendly inn also provides good disabled access and toilets, and special areas for non-smokers. The Salt Barge is open all day every day except in winter when it closes from 3pm to 5pm, Monday to Thursday. *The Salt Barge, Ollershaw Lane, Marston, nr Northwich, CW9 6ES. Tel: 01606 43064*

Lostock Gralam   Map 2 ref G4
2 miles E of Northwich on the A559

What a wonderful name for a relaxing pub: ***The Slow and Easy***. It could be referring to the bowls players on the manicured green that lies alongside. If you bowl yourself, you are welcome to use the green, free of charge, unless one of those very English, courteously lethal matches happens to be under way. In fact the inn's name, like that

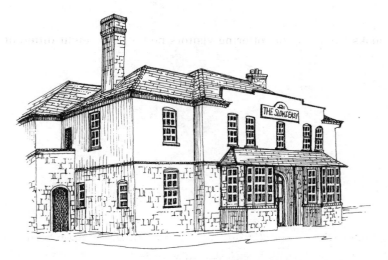

The Slow and Easy

of so many Cheshire pubs, comes from a race-horse who presumably wouldn't have been quite so famous if he had really lived up to his name. Dave and Cynthia Rowley run this popular pub located a couple of miles outside Northwich on the A559 road to Altrincham.

The Slow and Easy is open all day, everyday, and on weekday lunchtimes and early evenings offers a good choice of wholesome, reasonably-priced meals and snacks. Access for the disabled is easy and children will enjoy their own special play area. And, if you are looking for a bed and breakfast stay in the area, The Slow and Easy has en suite rooms available all year round. *The Slow and Easy, Manchester Road, Lostock Gralam, Northwich, CW9 7PJ. Tel: 01606 42148*

Louise Wheildon is a well-known member of the British Horse Society and at her **Riverbank Riding School** in Lostock Gralam equestrians will find a comprehensive and expert service. Around 18 horses and ponies are stabled here, between them furnishing suitable mounts for people of any age, size, or level of riding skill from complete beginners to professionals. Louise also provides livery, riding tuition, jumping, and riding for the disabled. Hacking sessions can be arranged for one, two or three hours, either through

Riverbank Riding School

the nearby open countryside, or you can travel by horse trailer to the great parks at Tatton or Marbury a few miles away. (Hard hats, of course, are available for hire). The school also boasts a large outdoor arena with an all weather surface and floodlights for winter evenings. An exceptionally friendly and knowledgeable staff make a visit here a pleasure, and you may well want to take advantage of the special offer: "Pay for four one-hour lessons, get the fifth one free". *Riverbank Riding School, Riverbank Farm, Hall Lane, Lostock Gralam, nr Northwich,   CW9 6DG. Tel: 01606 - 47955*

Davenham

Map 2 ref F4

2 miles S of Northwich on the A533

In summer, the outside of the **Oddfellows Arms** is as pretty a picture of a village pub as you could wish to see with its many colourful window boxes embellishing the mellow brick walls. Inside, it's equally inviting with lots of olde worlde beams and interesting bygones placed around the four separate rooms, - bar, snug, lounge and dining room. One particularly eye-catching display is the glass cabinet

The Oddfellows Arms

containing 35 model steam railway engines, mesmerising for train buffs but in fact everyone seems fascinated by them. Pat moved here in 1992 and has turned what was then a run down ale house into one of the most popular pubs in the area. Much of that success is due to her bubbly personality but the food on offer at the Oddfellows Arms has also played a large part. It's available every day from noon until 2pm, with a good choice of hearty, very reasonably priced meals, along with freshly made sandwiches and a children's menu. A special menu is served on Sundays when it's definitely a good idea to book ahead. *Oddfellows Arms, 1, Hartford Road, Davenham, Northwich, CW9 8JA. Tel: 01606 42022*

Winsford
Map 2 ref F5

6 miles S of Northwich on the A54

Winsford is another of the Cheshire salt towns which expanded greatly during the 19th century, swallowing up the old villages of Over and Wharton on opposite banks of the River Weaver. Two legacies of those boom years should be mentioned. One is **Christ Church** which was specifically designed so that it could be jacked up in the event of subsidence. The other is **Botton Flash**, a sizeable lake caused by subsidence but now a popular water recreation area for the town.

Foxwist Green
Map 2 ref F4

5 miles SW of Northwich on minor road off the A556 or A54

The Plough Inn is a very special "hidden place", secreted away down a No Through Road on top of Beauty Bank in the tiny hamlet of Foxwist Green, near Whitegate. Surrounded by fields, this unspoilt pub dating back to 1910 has two olde-worlde rooms, full of character and charm. An ideal setting in which to enjoy the quite outstanding choice of home made food provided by David Hughes at remarkably reasonable prices. The evening menu lists almost a dozen starters, including Smoked Salmon Cornet filled with prawns and mayonnaise, even more main courses of which four are vegetarian, and a sweet menu to drool over with such treats as Apple and Raspberry Pie and a mysterious one called "Choux Naughty Thing". Daily specials make your choice even more difficult. Well-kept ales and more than 40 different wines are available to complement your food

The Plough Inn

selection. The menu is served from noon until 2pm, and from 6pm until 9pm every day, (and on Sundays in the summer the kitchens are open all day). The menu also includes sandwiches, baguettes, salads and jacket potatoes. An additional summer attraction at The Plough is its well-tended beer garden where you'll find a feature rockery and, appropriately enough, a sturdy old vintage plough. Sorry, no children under the age of fourteen are allowed inside the pub. *The Plough Inn, Beauty Bank, Whitegate, nr Northwich, CW8 2BP. Tel: 01606 889455*

Hartford
Map 2 ref F4
2 miles SW of Northwich on the A559

No self-respecting 16th century house should be without its resident ghost and **Hartford Hall** has quite a sociable one, a nun who goes by the name of Ida. She is believed to have some connection with Vale Royal Abbey and has manifested herself on many occasions, perhaps seeking out the sister nuns who lived here when Hartford Hall was a nunnery. Mike and Margaret Livingstone-Evans, who run this splendid hotel set amidst four acres of landscaped gardens, have named the Nuns' Room in honour of Ida and this spacious

Hartford Hall Hotel

room has become a very popular venue for civil weddings ever since the hotel acquired its Civil Wedding Licence. For the special day, Hartford Hall can offer a complete package which includes a complimentary Bridal Suite complete with spa bath. The beautiful grounds and lake provide a perfect backdrop for wedding photographs. The hotel's excellent à la carte restaurant and its bar serving imaginative pub meals are both open to non-residents, but bookings are essential for Sunday lunchtime. All of Hartford Hall's twenty letting rooms are en-suite, two of them with spa baths, and all luxuriously furnished with every modern amenity. *Hartford Hall, 81, School Lane, Hartford, Northwich, CW8 1PW. Tel: 01606 75711 / Fax: 782285*

Cuddington
Map 2 ref E4

5 miles SW of Northwich off the A49

Cuddington is at the western end of the **Whitegate Way**, a pleasant rural walk of about 5 miles which follows the trackbed of the old railway that used to carry salt from the Winsford mines. There is a picnic site and car park at the former **Whitegate Station**.

At **Poplar Farm**, on the edge of Cuddington village, John and Wendy Clarkson offer a traditional farmhouse bed and breakfast. Parts of the old farmhouse, built in warm red brick, date back to the 17th century and evidence of this original, timber-framed building can still be seen in some of the inside walls. The Clarksons have lived here for some sixteen years, running the 120-acre livestock farm and welcoming visitors to their lovely home. There are two

Poplar Farm

rooms available, both warm, snug and well-appointed, with a shared bathroom. Breakfast is the real farmhouse variety: good, wholesome ingredients and plenty of them! The meal is served in an area beneath the impressive wooden staircase which is such a striking feature of the house. John and Wendy do not offer evening meals, but will happily provide packed lunches and filled flasks for your day out in the Cheshire countryside. The outstanding facilities at Poplar Farm make this an ideal base for exploring the northern part of the county and Chester itself. *Poplar Farm, Cuddington Lane, Cuddington, nr Northwich, CW8 2SZ. Tel: 01606 883985*

Map 2 ref E4
5 miles W of Northwich on the B5153

Crowton has many times been voted the Best Kept Village in Cheshire and its 18th century hostelry, **The Hare & Hounds**, enjoys a particularly scenic position in this appealing village. A sparkling stream runs through its gardens and here you'll also find a pleasant patio area and two popular pet goats, Honeysuckle and Parsley.

Joe and Pamela Nicholson run this charming pub which the Chester Chronicle hailed as one of the six best eating establishments in Cheshire. Joe is the chef and although his repertoire includes an

The Hare & Hounds

excellent choice of meat, poultry and vegetarian meals, he's even more famous for his fish dishes. Halibut, Dover and lemon sole, sea bream and sea bass, crab, salmon, hake - the market's best is delivered fresh each day and transformed into a memorable meal. The main restaurant is a stylish 1995 addition overlooking the gardens. If you want to eat here, booking is strongly advised: The full menu is served throughout the inn at lunchtime but only served in the restaurant at night. Wine is available by the glass or bottle, the beers include Greenalls and two guest ales and, as a final welcoming touch on chilly days, real open fires will greet you as you enter. *The Hare & Hounds, Station Road, Crowton, nr Northwich, CW8 2RN. Tel: 01928 788851*

CHAPTER FIVE
In and Around Knutsford

Tabley House, Knutsford

Chapter 5 - Area Covered

*For precise location of places please refer to the colour
maps found at the rear of the book.*

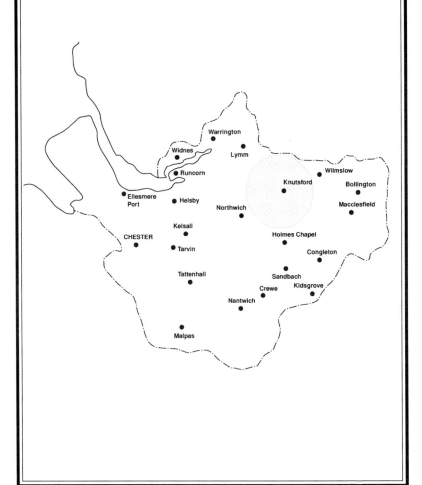

5
In and Around Knutsford

Introduction

Knutsford and its people were the heroes of one of the most durable of Victorian novels, Elizabeth Gaskell's *"Cranford"*. This gently humorous, sympathetic but sharply-observed portrait of the little Cheshire town, and the foibles and pre-occupations of its citizens, was first published in 1853 and it is still delighting readers today. Elizabeth was scarcely a month old when she came to Knutsford. Her mother had died shortly after her birth: her father sent her here to be brought up by an aunt who lived in a road which has now been re-named Gaskell Avenue. The motherless child grew up to be both strikingly beautiful and exceptionally intelligent. Early on she evinced a lively interest in the town's characters and its history. (She was intrigued, for example, to find that in the house next door to her aunt's had once lived a notorious highwayman, Edward Higgins, hanged for his crimes in 1767. She wrote a story about him). Marriage to William Gaskell, a Unitarian pastor in Manchester, took her away from Knutsford, although she returned often and for long periods, and after her death in 1865 was buried in the grounds of the Unitarian Chapel here.

Knutsford

The Knutsford that Elizabeth Gaskell knew so well and wrote about so vividly has expanded a great deal since those days of course, but in its compact centre, now designated an "outstanding area of conservation", the narrow streets and cobbled alleys still evoke the intimacy of a small Victorian town. Two parallel roads, Toft Street and King Street, form a rectangle surrounding the old town. But Mrs Gaskell would surely be astonished by the building erected in King Street to her memory by Mr Richard Harding Watt in 1907. A gifted entrepreneur, Mr Watt had made a huge fortune in Manchester as a glove manufacturer, but what really aroused his enthusiasm was the flamboyant architecture he had seen during his travels through Spain, southern Italy and the Near East.

On his return, he spent lavishly on trying to transform Knutsford in Cheshire into Knutsford-on-the-Mediterranean. At the north end of the town, he built a laundry complete with Byzantine domes and a minaret. A vaguely Ottoman style of architecture welcomed serious-minded artisans to his Ruskin Reading Rooms. In Legh Road, he erected a series of villas whose south-facing frontages are clearly in need of a really hot sun. And in King Street, as homage to the town's most famous resident, Richard Watt spent thousands of Victorian pounds on the *Gaskell Memorial Tower*. This tall, blank-walled building seems a rather incongruous tribute to the author who was herself so open and so down-to-earth.

Gaskell Memorial Tower

But it is eccentrics like Richard Watt who make English architecture as interesting as it is. He was so proud of his contribution to the town's new buildings that, travelling on his coach to the railway station, he would rise to his feet and raise his hat to salute them. As he did so, one day in 1913, his horse suddenly shied, the carriage overturned, and Richard Watt was thrown out and killed. What other changes he might have made to this grand old town, had he lived, we can only imagine.

Not far from the Gaskell Memorial Tower is the **Knutsford Wine Bar**, a magnificent restaurant housed in a fine old building dating back to the 18th century. In its time this building has been many things, including a fire station and a car show room, but since early 1992 has flourished as a wine bar and restaurant. The bar is open every day from 12 noon until 3pm for lunch/snacks and welcomes people just for coffee or drinks. (On Sundays, it opens at 11am for Bucks Fizz Breakfast, then there's lunch with live entertainment). Children are welcome at weekend lunchtimes. The bar re-opens every evening at 5.30pm (7pm on Sunday). The menu is very imaginative and interesting, using a wealth of ingredients from home and abroad. All the dishes are freshly prepared and delightfully garnished. The interior decor of the

Knutsford Wine Bar

wine bar mirrors the classy unpretentious exterior. On two levels with exposed brick walls, wooden floors and high ceilings, there is a wonderful spindled balustrade leading upstairs. With stylish live music on Tuesday and Thursday evenings, this is a wonderful place for lunch, an intimate dinner, or special party celebrations. *The Knutsford Wine Bar, 41a King Street, Knutsford, WA16 6DW. Tel: 01565 750459*

An unusual exhibition and well worth visiting is the **Penny Farthing Museum**, located in a courtyard off King Street. These bizarre machines were in fashion for barely twenty years before the last model was manufactured in 1892. The collection includes a replica of the famous *"Starley Giant"* with a front wheel 7ft in diameter.

Close by, in Tatton Street, is the **Knutsford Heritage Centre**. Knutsford is a town with a long history: - Edward I granted the town a Charter in 1262, (on August 3rd of that year, to be precise); at the same time, the local landowner, William de Tabley, was given a money-making licence to control the market. The Heritage Centre is housed in a restored 17th century timber-framed building which in Victorian times was a smithy and during the restoration, the old forge and bellows were found in a remarkable state of preservation.

The wrought iron gate in front of the centre was specially created for the Centre and depicts dancing girls taking part in Knutsford's famous Royal May Day celebrations - Royal because in 1887 the Prince and Princess of Wales honoured the festivities with their presence. Every May Day the town centre streets are closed to all traffic except for the May Queen's procession in which colourful characters such as *"Jack in Green"*, *"Highwayman Higgins"*, *"Lord Chamberlain"*, Morris and Maypole dancers, and many others take part. One curious tradition whose origins are unknown is the practice of covering the streets and pavements with ordinary sand and then, using white sand, creating elaborate patterns on top.

Princess Street also runs through the heart of old Knutsford and here you'll find **The Red Cow**, an imposing former coaching inn

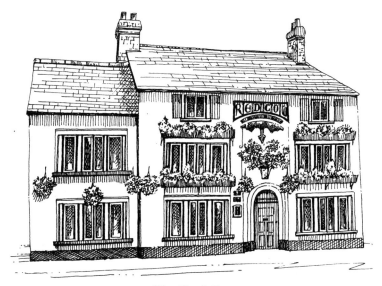

The Red Cow

dating back to the late 1700s. Ancient features like the splendid wooden floor, sturdy pillars and exposed brickwork blend happily with modern refurbishments to create a wonderful atmosphere. Similarly, the menu combines good old traditional pub favourites like the Ploughman's Platter, Giant Yorkshire Pud, bangers and mash, jacket potatoes and hot puddings, along with more adventurous dishes such as Chicken Jalfrezi served with Naan bread, mango chutney and a salad garnish. The Red Cow always offers at least two vegetarian choices and the daily specials board extends your options even further. Prices are extremely reasonable and, together with a fine range of top quality real ales and a good wine list, help explain why this welcoming inn is one of the most popular places in Knutsford for wining and dining. *The Red Cow, Princess Street, Knutsford, WA16 6BW. Tel: 01565 633408*

The old cobbled street that rises up to Knutsford's magnificent church is known as Church Hill and here you'll find **The Church Hill Gallery**. It is housed in a beautiful listed building, dating back

The Church Hill Gallery

to the 17th century, which for more than a century was a grocer's shop. Proud of the building's history, the Gallery's owners, Andrew and Sara Mount, have restored the vaulted ceiling in the cellar, where vinegar was once stored in vats, and designed solid oak fittings (inspired by the gothic atmosphere of the nearby church) to display their range of handmade gifts, interesting stationery, ribbons and giftwrap, and imaginative, unusual cards. These attractive items represent just one of the Gallery's three main enterprises. Upstairs is a well-presented collection of original paintings and limited edition prints with a special area dedicated to the work of the enigmatic artist, Graham Illingworth, whose distinctive creations in the tradition of Beardsley, Rackham and Erté have a devoted following. The Church Hill Gallery also offers a professional framing service, with two experienced craftsmen on hand to provide advice. *The Church Hill Gallery, Church Hill, Knutsford, WA16 6DH. Tel: 01565 633636*

Sweeping up to the very edge of Knutsford are the grounds of **Tatton Park**, 2,000 acres of exquisite parkland landscaped in the 18th century by the celebrated Humphrey Repton. This lovely park, where herds of red and fallow deer roam at will, provides a worthy setting for the noble Georgian mansion designed by the equally celebrated architect Samuel Wyatt. The combination of the two men's talents created a house and park that have become one of the National Trust's most visited attractions.

Tatton Park

Tatton's opulent staterooms, containing paintings by artists such as Canaletto and Van Dyck along with superb collections of porcelain and furniture, provided the television series Brideshead Revisited with a sumptuous setting for Marchmain House. More than 200 elegant pieces of furniture were commissioned from the celebrated cabinet-makers, Gillow of Lancaster. Particularly fine are the superb bookcases in the Library, constructed to house the Egerton family's collection of more than 8,000 books. By contrast, the stark servants' rooms and cellars give a vivid idea of what life below stairs was really like.

The Egerton family built Tatton Park to replace the much earlier **Old Hall** which nestles in a wood in the deer park and dates back to around 1520. Here, visitors are given a guided tour through time from the late Middle Ages up to the 1950s. Flickering light from candles reveals the ancient timber roof of the **Great Hall**, supported by ornate quatrefoils, while underfoot, the floor is strewn with rushes, providing a warm place for the medieval Lord of the Manor and his servants to sleep. There's much more: Home Farm is a working farm, but working as it did in the 1930s, complete with vintage machinery. Traditional crafts, (including pottery), stables and many farm animals provide a complete picture of rural life some sixty years ago.

Tatton's famous gardens include a Victorian maze, an orangery and fernery, a serene Japanese garden, American redwoods, and a splendid Italian terraced garden. There's also a busy programme of educational activities for children, an adventure playground, shops, and a restaurant. You can even get married in the sumptuous mansion and hold your reception either in the house itself, in the recently refurbished Tenants Hall which can cater for parties of up to 430, or in a marquee in the magnificent grounds. With so much on offer no wonder Tatton Park has been described as the most complete historic estate in the country. *Tatton Park, Knutsford, WA16 6QN. Tel: 01565 654822 (24 hours)*

Fryer's Roses

At **Fryer's Roses**, on the outskirts of Knutsford, more than half a million roses are grown each year. The fertile Cheshire soil and climate prove ideal for cultivating first-class, tough and hardy rose trees. This family business, run by Gareth Fryer whose grandfather established the nursery back in 1912, has a distinguished record of winning international awards, including the most prestigious of all, the *"Golden Rose of the Hague"*, for its lovely, coral coloured rose "Warm Wishes". The same hybrid tea rose also won the "All-America Rose Selection Award" for 1998. As well as selling a vast variety of roses from the 100 acre site, the garden centre shop also sells a large range of plants and goods, including dried and artificial flowers, indoor plants, troughs, pots and garden furniture. The splendid licensed coffee shop, with its patio for sunny days, has an outstanding regular menu and an ever-changing choice of daily specials. A selection of breakfasts is served throughout the morning; hearty brunches ("The Hungry Gardener", for example), salads, sandwiches, filled croissants and jacket potatoes, and the childrens' menu are available all day. Specially recommended is the enticing selection of home made cakes, pastries, pies and gâteaux. *Fryer's Roses, Manchester Road, Knutsford, WA16 0SX. Tel: 01565 755455*

Tabley
Map 3 ref G3

2 miles W of Knutsford on the A5033

Just to the west of Knutsford, on the A5033, is **Tabley House**, home of the Leicester family from 1272 to 1975. Mrs Gaskell often came to picnic in the grounds of the last of their houses, a stately Georgian mansion designed by John Carr for the first Lord de Tabley in 1761. This Lord de Tabley loved paintings and it was his son's passion for art, and his hunger for others to share it, which led to the

Tabley House

creation of London's National Gallery. His personal collection of English pictures, on display in Tabley House, includes work by Turner (who painted the house several times), Reynolds, Opie and Martin Danby, along with furniture by Chippendale, and fascinating family memorabilia spanning three centuries. The 17th century chapel next to the house looks perfectly in place but it was originally built on an island in Tabley Mere and only moved to its present site in 1927. (From April to the end of October, Tabley House is open in the afternoons, Thursday to Sunday, and on Bank Holidays).

Close by is **The Windmill Inn** but don't bother looking for a windmill in order to find it. This charming old hostelry, housed in a 16th century cottage, is actually named after a horse. Windmill the horse, a winner of the Chester Gold Cup, came from the stable of Lord D'Tabley of nearby Tabley Hall who, when he sold this cottage for use as a public house, insisted that it should be named after his favourite beast.

The Windmill Inn

The inn is a rambling old building with two dining-rooms (one apiece for smokers and non-smokers), other rooms with open fires and cosy nooks and corners where you can also take your meal, and three bed and breakfast rooms. Food is available at lunchtime and in the evening, every day, with a menu that offers hearty, traditional English meals along with vegetarian dishes such as Mushroom Balti and Spinach & Ricotta Tartellini. Although there's no windmill to guide you there, the inn is very easy to find since it stands beside the A556 near junction 19 of the M6. *The Windmill Inn, Chester Road, Tabley, Knutsford, WA19 0HW. Tel: 01565 632670*

Also in Tabley, at the Old School, is the **Tabley Cuckoo Clock Collection**. Brothers Roman and Maz Piekarski are well-known horologists and clock restorers and over the last 25 years they have sought out and renovated some of the rarest and most notable examples of this 300-year-old craft. Also on display are some mid-19th century cuckoo clocks which included complex musical movements to reproduce popular tunes of the day. For opening times, call 01565 633039.

Mere *Map 3 ref G3*

3 miles NW of Knutsford on the A50/A556

One of the **Kilton Inn's** more notorious guests, back in the 18th century, was Dick Turpin. The intrepid highwayman made this historic old inn the base from which he plundered travellers along the Knutsford to Warrington road (now the comparatively safe A50). After one such robbery (and murder) Turpin, on his famous horse Black Bess, *"galloped to the Kilton and, altering the clock, strolled on to the bowling green and proved an alibi by the short time he took to cover the four miles".*

The Kilton Inn

Nowadays, a more respectable clientele patronises this attractive inn, part of the Premier Lodge family of comfortable, hospitable, and value-for-money establishments. Flagstone floors, polished wood and intriguing memorabilia displayed around the rooms combine happily with such modern comforts as modem-compatible telephones, Sky TV and trouser-presses in each of the 28 en-suite bedrooms. The Kilton also offers an extensive menu that includes everything from simple snacks to an 8oz sirloin steak; a vegetarian gnocchi pomodoro to a traditional hot pudding. *The Kilton Inn, Warrington Road, Hoo Green, Mere, nr Knutsford, WA16 0PZ. Tel: 01565 830420*

High Legh
Map 3 ref G3
5 miles NW of Knutsford on the A50
High Legh Garden Centre, which celebrated its tenth anniversary in 1997, is one of the country's premier centres and conveniently placed near the motorway network. With plenty on offer this garden centre of excellence makes a great day out for all the family, whether they are expert gardeners or enthusiastic beginners. The nursery, with its numerous outdoor beds and covered areas, contains a wide variety of trees, plants and shrubs and, as a member of the Hillier Premier Plant Scheme enjoys access to more unusual outdoor plants. All are grown with great care and attention and the friendly, knowledgeable staff are on hand to help with any queries visitors have on the growing of their purchases.

Having the right tools for the job makes gardening much more of a pleasure and High Legh stocks all the leading brands of gardening equipment as well as a whole range of composts, chemicals and fertilisers to help create the perfect medium for the plants and

High Legh Garden Centre

shrubs. Situated to the rear of the nursery visitors will find a number of franchises which specialise in garden and home improvements, these include patios and driveways, conservatories, greenhouses and sheds and suppliers of turf and a specialist aquatic centre. To keep the children entertained there is also a safe and enjoyable outdoor play area.

Gardening is not all hard work and High Legh stocks an impressive range of garden furniture and accessories so that, after the work is over, gardeners can sit back and enjoy their labours. From attractive sun loungers and parasols to barbecues and fireworks, there is everything here to ensure that the garden becomes a place for peaceful relaxation. Also undercover is the Planthouse which, throughout the year contains a magnificent display of colourful and fragrant indoor plants that not only make the perfect gift but also brighten up any home or conservatory.

The delightful gift shop offers a superb range of unusual pottery, glassware, fragrant and aromatherapy products, speciality foods, designer knitwear, leisure clothing, greeting cards and gift wrappings, complemented by a comprehensive book department offering titles to suit all ages. For the young gardener there is an excellent range of garden toys and accessories from which to choose.

The changing seasons are reflected in the impressive and unusual displays seen at High Legh and towards Christmas the centre is transformed into a Winter Wonderland with glittering decorations, garlands, wreaths, Christmas trees of all shapes and sizes and a spectacular grotto where children can visit Father Christmas.

Any visit to High Legh would not be complete without a stop at the Greenhouse Cafe. Visitors can sit and relax with family and friends over a drink or delicious home-cooked meals and consider their next purchase whilst children can enjoy their favourite foods from the special children's menu. High Legh's commitment to excellence extends further to include a wide variety of special events they hold throughout the year which include informative and interesting demonstrations, talks, preview evenings and garden events. With extensive car parking, level site access and disabled facilities, High Legh Garden Centre is well worth a visit at any time of the year. *High Legh Garden Centre, High Legh, Knutsford, Cheshire WA16 0QW Tel: 01925 756991 Fax: 01925 757417*

Mobberley
Map 3 ref H3

2 miles E of Knutsford on the B5085

Mobberley village is scattered along the B5085, with its notable church set slightly apart. The main glory here is the spectacular woodwork inside: massive roof beams with striking winged figures and one of the finest rood screens in the country, dated 1500. The screen is covered with a rich tracery of leaves and fruit, coats-of-arms, and religious symbols. Two generations of the Mallory family held the rectorship here, one of them for 53 years. He is commemorated in the east window. Another window honours his grandson, George Mallory, the mountaineer who perished while making his third attempt to climb Mt Everest in 1924.

The Roebuck Inn is a lovely old coaching inn, its walls smothered with climbing plants. The inn dates back to the 17th century and its long history lives on in the oak beams, the panelled walls in the Library Room and the memorabilia scattered about the ancient rooms. The Roebuck stands on what used to be the main Knutsford to Alderley Edge road, - a much quieter thoroughfare now since the

THE ROEBUCK

The Roebuck Inn

bypass was opened. The inn is a free house, owned and personally run by Lin and David Robinson since 1995, and they make sure that they can always offer you at least six different beers. Three of them will be guest beers: permanently available are Boddingtons, Hydes and Marstons along with Guinness and Murphy's. Food is served every lunchtime and evening, and on Sundays from noon until 8.30pm. At weekends, if you want to eat in the dining room, please book ahead, but even without a booking you can eat in any of the Roebuck's rooms or in the pleasant Beer Garden. Children are welcome, there's good access for the disabled, and on Sunday evenings the entertainment includes music from the 60s and 70s and fun quizzes open to all. *The Roebuck Inn, Mill Lane, Mobberley, WA16 7XH. Tel: 01565 872757*

Just up the road from The Roebuck Inn is **Hillside Ornamental Fowl** which has twice won the award for the Best Small Tourist Attraction in the North West. Pools, waterfalls and gardens provide a pleasant habitat for a vast variety of birds from penguins to parrots. Hillside has now successfully bred more than 100 species of bird, some of them for the first time in Britain. If you have never heard a Kookaburra laugh, seen a Screamer, or ever wondered what a Curassow or a Wonga Wonga looks like, do pay a visit. Hillside also offers visitors a picnic area and a tea room .

The **Hinton Guest House** in Town Lane, Mobberley is the proud recipient of many awards and commendations from travel and tourist organisations. Built during the early 1960s, this detached property holds a lot more than would appear at first sight, - rather like Doctor Who's Tardis! The Hinton is owned and run by Joyce and Donald Read who extend a warm and friendly welcome to all guests whether on holiday or on business.

The Hinton Guest House

The six en-suite bedrooms are spacious and luxuriously furnished with a host of extras such as bathrobes and a beverage bar. Breakfast is served in the pretty dining room from 7.30 to 9.00am, and dinner between 6.00 and 7.00pm. The Hinton is licensed so you can also enjoy a drink with your meal. The comfortable guest lounge provides a perfect place to relax or you might even like to tickle the ivories of the organ here.

Another popular amenity is the splendid conservatory at the rear of the house which overlooks an eye-catching and well-tended garden. The Hinton is a quite exceptional guest house and conveniently located: Tatton Park is just five minutes drive away and the attractions of Chester, North Wales and the Peak District of Derbyshire are all within easy reach. *The Hinton Guest House, Town Lane, Mobberley, Knutsford, WA16 7HH. Tel: 01565 873484*

The Railway Inn in Mobberley is one of those lovely old pubs you know are out there somewhere, but can never be quite sure of finding. The Railway Inn is rather easier to find than most, since it's right next to Mobberley Station and signposted from the village. The building is over 200 years old: the welcome from its hosts, Lynda and Tony Davies, as warm and inviting as the inn itself. Tony is in charge of the bar and cellar: Lynda supervises a kitchen offering a

The Railway Inn

range of excellent bar snacks and evening meals, with scaled-down portions (and prices) for children. Lynda's dishes are attractively presented and very reasonably priced (perhaps even more enjoyable if your children have scampered off to their very own play area). A recent addition is a smart family dining room (non-smoking) overlooking the gardens at the rear. Tables here can be booked or you can enjoy your meal in any of the inn's comfortable and atmospheric rooms. *The Railway Inn, Station Road, Mobberley, WA16 6LA Tel: 01565 873155*

The Frozen Mop is situated in Faulkners Lane, Mobberley, just half a mile off the Mobberley to Wilmslow road. The building makes an appealing picture, parts of it dating back to the 18th century but with extensive more recent additions. The interior is splendid, full of character and charm, with wooden and flagstone floors, exposed brickwork and feature fireplaces to delight the eye. Attractively decorated and furnished, the Frozen Mop is a place for all the fam-

The Frozen Mop

ily with all the facilities to match. It is part of the Brewers Fayre chain of pubs so you can be confident of finding delicious, well-prepared food along with excellent, well-kept ale and a good choice of modestly-priced wines. If adults are well-provided for, children are positively pampered with their very own Charlie Chalk menu, a family room and a safe play area. *The Frozen Mop, Faulkners Lane, Mobberley, WA16 7AL. Tel: 01565 873234*

Great Warford   Map 3 ref H3
4 miles E of Knutsford on the B5085

Great Warford isn't Great at all, at least in size. Indeed, there aren't many maps which find space to include it. But it's certainly worthwhile seeking out this elusive village, halfway between Alderley Edge and Mobberley, in order to visit **The Stags Head**, a very "hidden place" run by William and Sylvia Anderson. Their hospitable inn, lost in picturesque Cheshire countryside, is far from unknown to local people who come here regularly to enjoy its welcoming atmosphere, lovely beer garden (with plenty of room for the kids to run around) and exceptionally good food. Outside, the former farmhouse

The Stags Head

looks like a picture with its many hanging baskets and window boxes: inside, features like the Victorian tiled fireplace surrounding a roaring fire welcome you to a very special, friendly place. Everything on the menu here is home cooked, whether it's a substantial Steak Pie or Chicken Curry, Pink Trout Fillets or Japanese Prawns. Enjoy your meal either inside this attractive pub, or on the cobbled patio at the back, surrounded by plants and shrubs. *The Stags Head, Mill Lane, Great Warford, Alderley Edge, SK9 7TY. Tel: 01565 872350*

Goostrey   *Map 3 ref H4*
6 miles S of Knutsford on minor road off A50
The village of Goostrey is a quiet little place on a minor road just north of Holmes Chapel but famous for its annual gooseberry shows where competitors vie to produce the plumpest berries.

Here you will find one of the most popular pubs in the area, **The Red Lion**. Real fires, candlelit tables in the dining-room, and a collection of gleaming copper hunting horns around the walls impart a very individual character to this hospitable inn run by Frank McCabe and David Howitt. The inviting dining-room has low beams and soft lighting, bookshelves stacked with real books and an intriguing display of ornaments and memorabilia. Food is served until 2pm at lunchtime, and until 9.30pm in the evenings. (At weekends, booking is advisable).

The Red Lion

The Red Lion's chef is Chinese so, although the lunchtime menu concentrates on mainly English dishes, in the evening along with those traditional meals, you can also take your pick from exotic Chinese, Indian and Middle Eastern delicacies, at least five of which will be vegetarian. The Red Lion also offers two large game rooms, a disco every other Sunday and, on most Fridays, a live band playing from 9pm. *The Red Lion, 3, Station Road, Goostrey, CW4 8PJ. Tel: 01477 532033*

Allostock   *Map 3 ref G4*
7 miles S of Knutsford on the A50
Hills Garden Centre has enjoyed half a century of success since it first opened its doors to discriminating gardeners. At that time dahlias were enormously popular, so Hills provided every possible variety of dahlia. As fashions in flowers changed, so did the plants cultivated in their seven acres of nursery grounds.

Nowadays, Hills specialises in winter and summer bedding plants, cyclamen (between 13 and 14,000 grown each year) and dwarf conifers, but this customer-friendly garden centre also offers a vast range of other natural products, - seeds, seedlings, shrubs, trees and established plants. You'll also find an equally generous choice of garden furniture, stonework, ornaments, sheds and conservatories. Experienced staff are on hand to offer advice on any gardening problem and it's a pleasure to wander around the well laid out dis-

Hills Garden Centre

play areas. Allow a good hour or so to see everything on offer at this exceptional garden centre which is open seven days a week, all year round. Hills is conveniently located on the A50 at Allostock, between Knutsford and Holmes Chapel. *Hills Garden Centre, London Road, Allostock, nr Knutsford, WA16 9LU. Tel: 01565 722567*

Lower Peover   *Map 3 ref G4*
4 miles S of Knutsford on the B5081

The village of Lower Peover (pronounced Peever) is effectively made up of two hamlets. One is grouped around the village green on the B5081, the other is at the end of a cobbled lane. It's a picturesque

The Bells of Peover

little group: a charming old coaching inn, **The Bells of Peover**, a handsome village school founded in 1710, and a lovely black and white timbered church, more than 700 years old. St Oswald's is notable as one of the few timber-framed churches in the country still standing.

Inside, there is a wealth of carved wood, - pews and screens, pulpit and lectern, and a massive medieval chest made from a single log of bog oak. At one time local girls who wished to marry a farmer were required to raise its lid with one hand to demonstrate they had the strength to cope with farm life. Former guests at The Bells of Peover have included Generals Patton and Eisenhower during World War II, and the American flag still flies here alongside the Union Jack.

The pub was noted then for its food, and today this charming old building, run by Ken and Wendy Brown, has again become one of the most famous eating places in the country, celebrated for its truly distinguished menu. (At weekends, if you wish to eat in the dining room, do book ahead). Although the pub is so close to St Oswald's, it is not the church bells which gave the pub its name but a 19th century licensee, a Mr Bell. He was here for so many years that locals came to refer to his hostelry as simply "Bells", rather than by its official name, *"The Warren de Tabley Arms"*. *The Bells of Peover, The Cobbles, Lower Peover, nr Knutsford, WA16 9PZ. Tel: 01565 722269*

Also to be found in Lower Peover is **The Crown**, a splendid 17th century inn as inviting outside, with its cream-painted walls and hanging baskets, as it is inside where Lesley and Bert Flint have decorated the rooms with a wide variety of artefacts and memorabilia collected over many years. The Flints have been "mine hosts" here for a quarter of a century and have maintained The Crown's reputation for good food and drink along with a warm and friendly welcome throughout that time. Food is available every day at both lunchtime and in the evening and the excellent menu offers a wide choice of starters, old favourites such as Steak & Kidney Pie, light

The Crown

bites, fish and vegetarian dishes, all attractively presented and reasonably priced. The Crown's real ales, served in prime condition,
include Boddingtons, Flowers and Trophy, as well as a varying choice
of three guest ales. Children are welcome and there is good access
for the disabled. *The Crown, Crown Lane, Lower Peover, WA16 9QB.
Tel: 01565 722074*

About 3 miles east of Lower Peover is **Peover Hall**, very much
hidden away at the end of a winding country road but well worth
tracking down. During World War II, General George Patton lived
for a while at the Hall which was conveniently close to his then
headquarters at Knutsford. There's a memorial to him in the church
nearby, but many many more to the Mainwaring family whose fine
monuments crowd beside each other in both the north and south
chapels. (Please note that the Hall is only open to the public on
Monday afternoons between May and October).

Plumley *Map 3 ref G4*
4 miles SW of Knutsford off the A556

As its slogan says, **The Hidden Nursery** is indeed *"a gem worth
finding"*. To find it, seek out the village of Plumley, about a mile off
the A556 between Knutsford and Northwich. The nursery has been
located here for more than half a century, providing gardeners with
a comprehensive range of plants, shrubs and trees of every colour,
shape and size. Aidan Killeen and his staff have developed the nursery into a Mecca for gardeners and have built on the nursery's already
excellent reputation. In addition to the huge choice on offer, the

The Hidden Nursery

centre also specialises in specimen plants, - the larger, more mature and distinctive plants that make an immediate impact on your garden. You'll also find every possible kind of garden accessory on display here: seeds, composts, tools, garden ornaments and decorative pots in abundance - to name just a few items. If you are looking for a special plant for the garden, you will surely find it at The Hidden Nursery. Experienced staff are always on hand to give seasoned advice on any gardening query or problem you may have. The Hidden Nursery is open from 9am to 6pm every day and, during the season, there's a Coffee Shop which is open at weekends. *The Hidden Nursery, Plumley Moor Road, Plumley, Knutsford, WA16 9SD. Tel: 01565 722315*

CHAPTER SIX
In and Around Macclesfield

Gawsworth Hall

Chapter 6 - Area Covered

For precise location of places please refer to the colour maps found at the rear of the book.

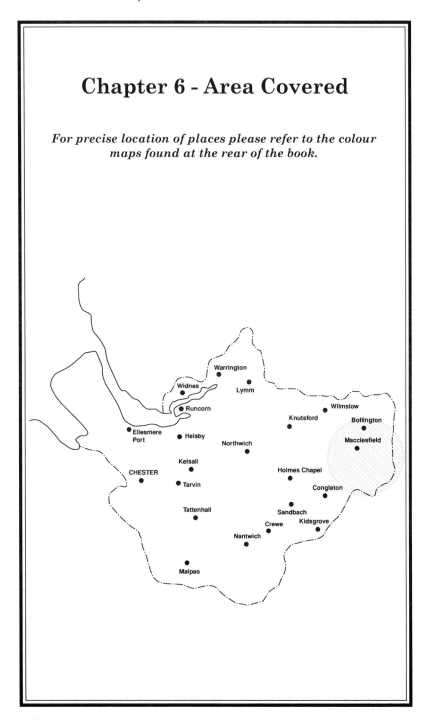

6
In and Around Macclesfield

Macclesfield

Nestling below the hills of the High Peak, Macclesfield was once an important silk manufacturing town. Charles Roe built the first silk mill here, beside the River Bollin, in 1743 and for more than a century and a half, Macclesfield was known as the silk town. It's appropriate then that Macclesfield can boast the country's only **Silk Museum** where visitors are given a lively introduction to all aspects of the silk industry, from cocoon to loom. The museum has an award-winning audio-visual presentation, there are fascinating exhibitions on the Silk Road across Asia, on silk cultivation, fashion and other uses of silk.

The silk theme continues at nearby **Paradise Mill**. Built in the 1820's, it is now a working museum demonstrating silk weaving on 26 jacquard hand looms. Exhibitions and restored workshops and living rooms capture the working conditions and lives of mill workers in the 1930s. It is also possible to buy locally-made silk products here. The Silk Museum is housed in what used to be the Macclesfield Sunday School, erected in 1813. The school finally closed in 1970 and the Silk Museum now shares this rather grand building with the town's **Heritage Centre** which has some interesting displays on Macclesfield's rich and exciting past, (the town was occupied for five days by Scottish troops during the Jacobite Rebellion of 1745, for example), and on the Sunday School itself.

In pre-Saxon times, Macclesfield was known as "Hameston", - the homestead on the rock, and on that rock is set the church founded by King Edward I and Queen Eleanor. From the modern town, a walk to the church involves climbing a gruelling flight of 108 steps. St Michael and All Angels was extended in the 1890's but its 14th century core remains, notably the **Legh Chapel** built in 1422 to receive the body of Piers Legh who had fought at Agincourt and died at the Siege of Meaux. Another chapel contains the famous Legh Pardon brass, which recalls the medieval practice of selling pardons for sins past, and even for those not yet committed. The inscription on the brass records that, in return for saying five Paternosters and five Aves, the Legh family received a pardon for 26,000 years and 26 days.

As its name suggests, **Abaraginals Café Bar** has an Australian theme, the first enterprise of its kind ever to open in Macclesfield. The owner, David Healey, was inspired to create this unique café

Abariganals Café Bar

bar following a visit to Australia and the wicker, colonial style furniture, Australian bric à brac and pictures from Down Under give Abariginals a refreshingly different atmosphere. Naturally, there are Australian beers on offer and the menu even includes kangaroo and crocodile meat in burgers, pies, kebabs and curries.

Open every day, Abaraginals is personally run by David Healey whose wife, Gill, looks after the more traditional **Porter's Ale House** just a couple of hundred yards away in Roe Street, opposite the Heritage Centre. Formerly the Prince of Wales pub, Porter's serves

Porter's Ale House

fine cask ales, always changing, and an excellent choice of lunch-time food. "Oven bottoms" are the speciality: large, fresh breadcakes baked on the oven bottom, served with a hearty hot filling of your choice, including vegetarian options. The atmosphere is appealingly olde-worlde with part-panelled walls, wooden ceilings and an intriguing array of bygones and memorabilia. *Abariginals Café, 27, Pickford Street, Macclesfield, SK11 6JD. Porter's Ale House, 33, Roe Street, Macclesfield, SK11 6UT. Tel: 01625 424796*

Curiously, Macclesfield has another connection with Australia in the form of William Buckley who was born here around 1780 and later became a soldier. He took part in a mutiny at Gibraltar against the Rock's commanding officer, (the father-to-be of Queen Victoria, as it happened). The mutiny failed and Buckley was transported to Australia. There he escaped into the outback and became the leader of an aboriginal tribe who took this giant of a man, some 6 feet 6 inches tall, as the reincarnation of a dead chief. For 32 years Buckley never saw a white man or heard a word of English. When the explorer John Bateman, on his way to found what is now Melbourne, discovered him, Buckley had virtually forgotten his mother tongue. He was pardoned, given a pension and died at Hobart at the age of 76.

Just two minutes walk from the town centre, **The British Flag** is believed to be the only pub with this name in the country. The

Union Jack hangs proudly on the signboard and also flutters from the tall flagpole high above. Built in 1860, this is a very traditional pub, its three separate rooms all Victorian in style. Lloyd and Viv Roberts run this friendly hostelry where the speciality of the house is its well-kept beer - indeed, The British Flag has received the accolade of an entry in the 1998 Good Beer Guide.

The British Flag

The other serious interest here is sport. The pub has its own football team and golf society, and every evening locals and visitors join in games of pool, cribbage, dominoes and skittles. And for special sporting events, there's a large screen television. This is purely a wet pub, so no food is available, and it is only open in the evenings from 5.30pm and on Sunday lunchtimes. There is good access for wheelchairs, but children are not permitted. *The British Flag, 42, Coare Street, Macclesfield, SK10 1DW. Tel: 01625 425500*

One of the Macclesfield area's most famous sons is Charles Frederick Tunnicliffe, the celebrated bird and wild-life artist, who was born at the nearby village of Langley in 1901. He studied at the Macclesfield School of Art and first came to public attention with his illustrations for Henry Williamson's *"Tarka the Otter"* in 1927.

A collection of Tunnicliffe's striking paintings can be seen at the **West Park Museum** on the northwest edge of the town. This purpose-built museum, founded in 1898 by the Brocklehurst family, also includes exhibits of Egyptian artefacts, fine and decorative arts. West Park Museum is on Prestbury Road and further along this road is **Upton House**, a grand Victorian detached house set in almost an acre of gardens. It was built around 1885 by a prosperous Macclesfield merchant who decided to build a house on the outskirts of the town that would reflect his wealth and his substantial position in society. John and Shirley Davies live here now and welcome

Upton House

visitors for bed and breakfast in their impressive but very welcoming house. (There's even a swimming pool in the garden which guests are free to make use of during the summer months). Upton House can accommodate a maximum of six guests in its four bedrooms, two of them en-suite, one with its own private bathroom. You reach your bedroom by way of a magnificent wooden staircase, an original feature of the house. Breakfast, (English or Continental), is served in a charming room overlooking the attractive, secluded garden. Children are welcome, smoking is permitted, but because of the staircase approach to the bedrooms, the house is not suitable for the disabled. *Upton House, 156, Prestbury Road, Macclesfield, SK10 3BR. Tel: 01625 619514*

Also a short distance from the West Park Museum is **Mayfield**, and if you are planning to stay anywhere in the Macclesfield area, then this is an ideal place for bed and breakfast. This grand old house was built in 1870, a time when the Victorians certainly knew how to build spacious, comfortable dwellings in which you immediately feel at home. Ruth Parker, who owns this lovely house built in warm, red-tinted brick, has been welcoming guests since 1995, many

Mayfield

of them returning year after year. There are two letting rooms: one twin, one single, both sharing a bathroom. The old-fashioned beds and vintage furniture are particularly appealing, and if you enjoy a hearty breakfast you will be well-pleased at Mayfield. As one visitor remarked after finishing his breakfast here, "I don't think I'll be needing lunch". You might want an evening meal however, and Ruth will be happy to provide it, just let her know. Children are welcome, but the stairs make the house difficult for the disabled and smoking is not permitted. *Mayfield, 25, Victoria Road, Macclesfield, SK10 3JA. Tel: 01625 613068*

To the east of the town centre runs the **Macclesfield Canal**, one of the highest waterways in England, running for much of its length at more than 500 ft above sea level. Thomas Telford was the surveyor of the 26-mile long route, opened in 1831, which links the **Trent & Mersey** and the **Peak Forest** canals. Between Macclesfield and Congleton, the canal descends over a hundred feet in a spectacular series of 12 locks at Bosley, before crossing the River Dane via Telford's handsome iron viaduct. Other unusual features of this superbly-engineered canal are the two *"roving bridges"* south of Congleton. These swing from one bank to the other where the towpath changes sides and so enabled horses to cross over without having to unhitch the tow-rope.

Prestbury
Map 3 ref I3

3 miles N of Macclesfield via the A523/A538

A regular winner of the Best Kept Village title, Prestbury is a charming village where a tree-lined High Street runs down to a bridge over the River Bollin, ancient stocks stand against the church wall, old coaching inns and black and white buildings mingle with the mellow red brick work of later Georgian houses.

The **Church of St Peter**, dating from the 13th century, still maintains a tradition which began in 1577. Every autumn and winter evening at 8pm a curfew bell is rung, with the number of chimes corresponding to the date of the month. Close by is a building known as the **Norman Chapel** with a striking frontage carved with the characteristic Norman zig-zags and beaked heads. Even older are the carved fragments of an 8th century Saxon cross preserved under glass in the graveyard. Opposite the church is a remarkable magpie timber-framed house which is now a bank but used to be the Vicarage. During the Commonwealth, the rightful incumbent was debarred from preaching in the church by the Puritans. Undaunted, the priest addressed his parishioners from the tiny balcony of his Vicarage.

Ye Olde Admiral Rodney inn stands on Prestbury's main street, close to the River Bollin. The building dates back to the late 17th century and before becoming an inn was part of a row of cottages,

Ye Olde Admiral Rodney

and then a brewhouse. Full of character and charm, befitting a building of such great age, Ye Olde Admiral Rodney is a traditional English village inn where you can be sure of finding good ale, good food and good company. The olde worlde atmosphere is enhanced by a magnificent display of vintage ceramic Pirate Pots, a striking collection of commemorative plaques from old boats and regiments, and a lovely old ship's wheel. Managed by Gail and Peter Brady, the inn serves meals from 12 noon -2.30pm, Monday to Saturday, and children are welcome to come and eat here. Once visited, Ye Olde Admiral Rodney with its well-kept ales and wonderful atmosphere, is a pub that you will want to return to time and time again. *Ye Olde Admiral Rodney, Prestbury, Macclesfield, SK10 4HP. Tel: 01625 828078*

Bollington Cross   *Map 3 ref I3*
3 miles N of Macclesfield via A523/B5090

One of the family of Greenalls Bygone Inns, **The Cock and Pheasant** at Bollington Cross dates back to 1780. As you step inside this ancient inn, it's easy to imagine yourself living in those less stressful times. Low, beamed ceilings, wooden floors, a wealth of old artefacts (almost a complete vintage wash-house in one corner), - once you've settled at your table, you'll be reluctant to leave.

The Cock and Pheasant

Your hosts, Agostinho and Maureen de Freitas, who have been together in the catering business for more than thirty years, would be equally sorry to see you go without sampling at least one of the many choices from their menu, beautifully inscribed in immaculate chalk handwriting on two huge blackboards. The emphasis is on traditional English food (toad in the hole, cod with mushy peas, bread and butter pudding, or sherry trifle) but with some continental flourishes such as seafood au gratin, or prawn, avocado and smoked salmon salad. If your travels around Cheshire take you anywhere near Bollington Cross, do go the extra few miles to seek out the Cock & Pheasant. *The Cock and Pheasant, 15, Bollington Road, Bollington Cross, nr Macclesfield, SK10 5EJ. Tel: 01625 573289*

Bollington   Map 3 ref I3
4 miles NE of Macclesfield on the B5091

In its 19th century heyday, there were 13 cotton mills working away at Bollington, a little town perched on the foothills of the High Peak. Two of the largest mills, the Clarence and the Adelphi, still stand, although now adapted to other purposes. The Victorian shops and cottages around Water Street and the High Street recall those busy days. A striking feature of the town is the splendid 20-arched viaduct which once carried the railway over the River Dean. It is now part of the **Middlewood Way** a ten mile, traffic-free country trail which follows a scenic route from Macclesfield to Marple. The Way is open to walkers, cyclists and horse riders and during the season cycles are available for hire, complete with child seats if required. Just as remarkable as the viaduct, although in a different way, is **White Nancy**, a round stone tower which stands on **Kerridge Hill**, more than 900ft above sea level. It was built to commemorate the Battle of Waterloo and offers sweeping views in all directions

   Mauro's Italian restaurant, on the main street in the heart of Bollington village, features in many of the good restaurant guides. Well known in the area, this restaurant provides an authentic taste

Mauro's Italian Restaurant

of Italy in the heart of rural England. Owned and personally run by chef Enzo Mauro, this is the place to come to for a sophisticated lunch or dinner in intimate and cosy surroundings. The food, as you would expect, is out of this world. The house specialities include home made pasta, fish dishes, and the wonderful puddings and sweets. As well as the extensive menu there's always a couple of daily specials that make use of the freshest ingredients from the markets. There is a super wine list with over 60 labels to choose from, ranging from the classical to New World vineyards, and also the largest selection of grappas to be found in the north west. *Mauro's, 88, Palmerston Street, Bollington, nr Macclesfield, SK10 5PW. Tel: 01625 573898*

Pott Shrigley   Map 3 ref I3
6 miles NE of Macclesfield on minor road off the B5091 or B5470

Pott Shrigley is a tiny village just inside the Peak District National Park. **The Coffee Tavern**, about a mile from the centre of the village, has had a very checkered history. It was built in 1887 as a Reading Room and Library for employees of the Lowther family's estate nearby. The estate staff seem to have lost their interest in improving literature by the end of the first World War and their Reading Room was then converted into a tea room. The second World War put an end to that particular venture also but this characterful old building with its two Minstrels' Galleries is now, once again, very much in business.

The Coffee Tavern

The Buffey family who have run The Coffee Tavern since 1992 offer their guests a menu that includes everything from a single cup of tea to a three-course meal. The regular menu (available every day from 10am to 6pm) is supplemented by at least six daily specials listed on the blackboard. If you are looking for local crafts, The Coffee Tavern is an excellent place to start your search: here you will find a remarkable selection of paintings, jewellery, pottery, dried flowers and much more, all created by artists who live and work nearby. *The Coffee Tavern, Shrigley Road, Pott Shrigley, nr Macclesfield, SK10 5SE. Tel: 01625 576370*

Rainow   Map 3 ref J4

3 miles NE of Macclesfield on the A5002

Situated on the edge of the Peak District National Park, **The Country Café** is also very close to Nab Head, the hill-top vantage point offering spectacular views across east Cheshire. And not far away is White Nancy, a round stone tower from whose summit, 920ft above sea level, there are equally astonishing vistas westwards into Lancashire, eastwards to the Derbyshire hills.

The Country Café

The Country Café itself is hidden away on a minor road leading from Bollington to Pott Shrigley. It's a pleasing one-storey building which has been welcoming customers for more than half a century and, remarkably, during those fifty years, the café has only had two owners. The present hosts are Edwin and Kathleen Green (assisted by their daughter Lesley) who came here in July 1997 and speedily acquired a reputation for delicious home made and home cooked food. From 12.30pm to 2pm they offer either a 3-course lunch or individual dishes such as plaice or scampi. They're open again from 3.30pm until 6pm when the menu also includes Afternoon and High Teas. It's well worth seeking out this cosy, quaint, (and no-smoking) café where children are welcome and disabled access is easy. *The Country Café, Spuley Lane, Rainow, nr Macclesfield. SK10 5DE. Tel: 01625 573357*

Sutton   Map 3 ref I4

2 miles S of Macclesfield on minor road off the A523

This small village, close to the Macclesfield Canal, is honoured by scholars as the birthplace of Raphael Holinshed whose famous *"Chronicles"* provided the source material for no fewer than 14 of Shakespeare's plays. As well as drawing heavily on the facts in the Chronicles, the Immortal Bard wasn't above plagiarising some of Holinshed's happier turns of phrase.

Blossom Cottage was built around 1880 for the housekeeper and gardener of the nearby estate of Sutton Oaks. The house is as appealing as its name, with beams and old-style leaded windows and a warm, inviting appearance. Dave and Rita Caveney only let out one room at the moment, a double with its own bathroom next door, so their guests get very well looked after indeed! The room itself is very warm and cosy with lots of olde-worlde charm, but at

Blossom Cottage

the same time also provides all the modern amenities - even Sky TV. A second room available soon will include a four-poster bed. The very reasonable tariff includes of course a hearty English breakfast. Blossom Cottage is an ideal spot from which to explore this part of Cheshire, the High Peak district of Derbyshire and the Staffordshire moorlands. To find the cottage, take the A523 out of Macclesfield towards Leek and when you come to the Fools Nook pub, turn left into Radcliffe Road. Blossom Cottage is the second house on your left. *Blossom Cottage, 2, Radcliffe Road, Sutton, Macclesfield, SK11 0JE. Tel: 01260 252903*

Warren

Map 3 ref I4

3 miles SW of Macclesfield on the A536

Just outside the village of Warren is **Gawsworth Hall**, a captivating picture with its dazzling black and white half-timbered walls and lofty three-decker Tudor windows. The Hall was built in 1480 by the Fitton family, one of whose descendants, the celebrated beauty, Mary Fitton is believed to be the *"Dark Lady"* of Shakespeare's sonnets. The Bard would no doubt approve of Gawsworth's famous open-air theatre where performances range from his own plays to

Gawsworth Hall

Gilbert and Sullivan operas with the Hall serving as a lovely backdrop. Surrounded by a huge park, Gawsworth, to quote its owner Timothy Richards, *"is the epitome of a lived-in historic house"*. Every room that visitors see (which is virtually every room in the house) is in daily use by him and his family. And what wonderful rooms they are. Myriad windows bathe the rooms in light, the low ceilings and modest dimensions radiate calm, and even the richly-carved main staircase is conceived on a human scale. The beautifully sited church, and the lake nearby, add still more to the appeal of this magical place. The Hall is open every afternoon during the season, at other times by appointment. Tel: 01260 223456.

Lower Withington

Map 3 ref H4

7 miles W of Macclesfield on the B5392

Visible from miles around, the huge white dish of the world famous **Jodrell Bank** radio telescope has a good claim to being the most distinctive building in the county. The Observatory came into service in 1957 and was used by both Americans and the Soviets in their exploration of space. Its Science Centre offers visitors a wonderful array of hands-on exhibits, including a 25ft telescope, while its Planetarium transports through the heavens, explaining the secrets of

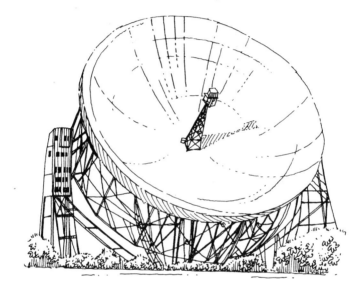

Jodrell Bank Radio Telescope

Rocky Dwarfs and Gassy Giants along the way. Albert Einstein and Isaac Newton are at hand to guide visitors on this fascinating exploration of the Universe. Outside, there's a superb 35-acre Arboretum planted with 2,500 species of trees and shrubs, each one helpfully labelled. Tel: 01477 571339.

Old farm buildings, sympathetically converted, provide the perfect setting for **Welltrough Dried Flowers** in the village of Lower Withington. The extensive buildings house one of the largest selections of dried and silk flowers in the North. There is a permanent Christmas Room, Dickensian Street and Demonstration Room where national demonstrator Barry Grey gives demonstrations and Day Workshops. As Welltrough is a working farm during the winter, the

Welltrough Dried Flowers

cows come into the barns to have their calves, and children are invited to name the new arrivals. There is so much to see that visitors are advised to allow at least one hour for their visit.

Welltrough is signed off the A535 Chelford to Holmes Chapel road. *Welltrough Dried Flowers, Welltrough Hall Farm, Lower Withington, nr Macclesfield, SK11 9EF Tel: 01477 571616*

Just half a mile up the road from Welltrough Dried Flowers is a gem of a pub, ***The Black Swan***. An attractive, white-painted building parts of which date back to the 16th century, it's located in Trap Street, named after the pub's age-old nickname of *"The Trap"* and the unusual extension to the pub is called *"The Trap Bar"*. This bar is worth visiting just to see its wonderful umbrella-style wooden roof, supported by a central wooden post, and reminiscent of the old mill roofs that were once common in this part of Cheshire.

The Black Swan

Another very good reason for visiting Graham and Judith Holland's superb hostelry is to sample the quality of the food along with the warm and friendly service, all of which they are so well renowned for. Graham leads a team of chefs in the kitchen and revels in creating inventive and imaginative dishes along with regular favourites. There's a full à la carte menu, the dishes changing daily, as well as a selection of "Pub Grub" and sandwiches, all of which are displayed on blackboards around the room. In addition, there are specials on offer to add to your choice, ranging from Sea Bass to Suckling Pig, from Sole Fillets to Pheasant. There is also an excellent wine list offering an extremely well-chosen selection of very good wines at reasonable prices. The Black Swan serves food at lunchtime and evening, and the restaurant is divided into smoking and non-smoking areas. *The Black Swan, Trap Street, Lower Withington, Macclesfield, SK11 9EQ. Tel: 01477 - 571602*

Chelford   *Map 3 ref H4*
6 miles W of Macclesfield on the A537

When Chelford's "local" was built in the late 1700's, it was respectfully named **The Egerton Arms** in deference to those great landowners in the area, the Egertons of Tatton Park, a few miles up the road. In those early days, the Egerton Arms was a simple ale house brewing its own beer using water from a well in the garden. Today, it still serves excellent, full-bodied ales but also a quite astonishing choice of food. The regular menu offers almost fifty different starters, main courses and desserts, then there's a snack list and a large selection of daily specials. Options range from the

The Egerton Arms

deliciously simple, a filled hot hob or a ploughman's, say, to hearty steaks and the house specialty, fish dishes like the marinated salmon fillet mesquite. No wonder Lee and Katrina Russell's hostelry has been featured in "The Enlightened Imbiber & Gourmet's Guide to the World's Greatest Pubs". With the extra attraction of extensive grounds where there is additional seating, The Egerton Arms is definitely an inn not to be missed. *The Egerton Arms, Knutsford Road, Chelford, SK11 9BB. Tel: 01625 861132*

Nether Alderley   Map 3 ref H3
6 miles NW of Macclesfield on the A34

The village of Nether Alderley lies on the A34 and here you will find **Nether Alderley Mill**, a delightful 15th century watermill that has been restored by the National Trust. The red sandstone walls are almost hidden under the huge sweep of its stone tiled roof. Inside is the original Elizabethan woodwork and Victorian mill machinery

Nether Alderley Mill

which is still in working order, with two tandem overshot wheels powering the mill. Nether Alderley Mill is open to the public on Wednesday and Sunday afternoons in April, May & October, and every afternoon except Monday from June to September. If you have time, visit the 14th century church of St Mary with its unusual richly carved pew, set up on the wall like an opera box and reached by a flight of steps outside. *Nether Alderley Mill, Nether Alderley, nr Alderley Edge, Macclesfield Tel: 01625 523012*

Very few garden centres anywhere can match the longevity of **Alderley Park Nurseries** which was founded more than 60 years

Alderley Park Nurseries

ago by Fred Matthews. The Matthews family still run the business. His daughters, Margaret and Wendy, Wendy's husband Iain, along with their children Nova, Alex and Kim, are all involved in this enterprising family firm. They have 30 acres of growing nursery stock and were pioneers in "containerising" trees and shrubs for out-of-season planting.

The choice here is phenomenal but if you feel in need of advice, the experienced staff will be happy to oblige, or you could take advantage of Alderley Park's landscaping service which will design and build anything from a patio garden to a five-acre plot. Wendy specialises in the floristry side of the business, providing floral arrangements for every kind of function and also offering brides-to-be a special bridal room where they can discuss their floral requirements in privacy and comfort. Yet another attraction at Alderley Park is its spacious, well-designed Coffee Shop serving beverages, cakes and light meals every day from 10am until 5pm; the Nursery itself is open daily from 9am until 6pm. *Alderley Park Nurseries, Nether Alderley, Macclesfield, SK10 4TH. Tel: 01625 582087*

Alderley Edge
Map 3 ref H3

6 miles NW of Macclesfield on the A34

Alderley Edge takes its name from the long, wooded escarpment, nearly two miles long, that rises 600 ft above sea level and culminates in sandy crags overlooking the Cheshire Plain. In Victorian times, this spectacular area was the private preserve of the Stanley family and it was only under great pressure that they grudgingly allowed the *"Cottentots"* of Manchester access on occasional summer weekends. It was the Stanley daughters who took great umbrage when the Wizard Inn hung up a new sign. They demanded its removal. The Merlin-like figure depicted could, they claimed, be taken as a representation of their father, Lord Stanley, at that time a virtual recluse and more than a little eccentric. Nowadays, however, walkers can roam freely along the many footpaths through the woods, one of which will take them to **Hare Hill Gardens**, a little known National Trust property. These Victorian gardens include fine woodland, a walled garden themed in blue, white and yellow flowers, and huge banks of rhododendrons. There is access by way of gravel paths for the less able.

The view from Alderley Edge over the Cheshire plain is one of the county's most memorable sights, and **The Alderley Edge Hotel**, just a short stroll away, is equally remarkable. It's a beautiful sandstone building, originally built in 1850 as the private home of one of Manchester's wealthy cotton barons. Lovingly and sympathetically refurbished, it is now recognised as one of the finest Country House Hotels in Britain with magnificent public rooms and luxuriously appointed bedrooms, eleven of which feature whirlpool tubs. The day starts well as you wake to the appetising aroma of freshly baked croissants, brioches and Danish pastries rising from the hotel bakery which also produces an amazing selection of breads, cakes and pastries every day. Lunch can be either a light meal in

Alderley Edge Hotel

the superb conservatory with its enviable views over Alderley Edge, or a fixed price or à la carte lunch in the Egon Ronay commended restaurant where dinner is also served until 10pm. Fresh fish from Fleetwood market arrives each morning; herbs come from the hotel's own gardens. The hotel is a delight for the gourmet, and also for the serious imbiber, with a wine list featuring 200 champagnes and 1,000 wines, as well as a breathtaking collection of fine malt whiskies. A truly outstanding hotel, open to non-residents for lunch, afternoon tea and dinner every day. *The Alderley Edge Hotel, Macclesfield Road, Alderley Edge, SK9 7BJ. Tel: 01625 583033*

CHAPTER SEVEN
Northwest Cheshire

Dunham Massey Hall

Chapter 7 - Area Covered

For precise location of places please refer to the colour maps found at the rear of the book.

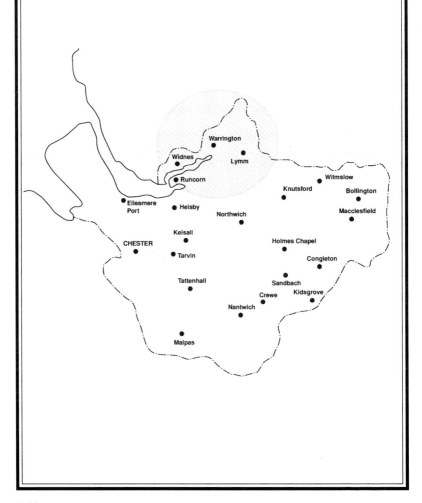

7
Northwest Cheshire

Warrington

Warrington is North Cheshire's largest town, - an important industrial centre since Georgian and Victorian times and with substantial
buildings of those days to prove it. Its imposing Town Hall was formerly Lord Winmarleigh's country residence, built in 1750 with all
the appropriate grandeur: windows framed in painfully expensive
copper, and elaborately-designed entrance gates 25ft high and 54ft
wide. Along with its park, it provides a dignified focus for the town
centre. A major Victorian contribution to the town is its excellent
Museum and **Art Gallery** in Bold Street, one of the earliest mu-
nicipal museums dating from 1857. The exhibits are remarkably
varied: amongst them are shrunken heads, a unique china teapot
collection, a scold's bridle, Egyptian mummies, a Roman actor's mask
and other Roman artefacts discovered in nearby Wilderspool. There
are some fine paintings as well, most of which are Victorian water-
colours and oils, and a rare Vanous still life. An interesting curiosity
at **Bridge Foot** nearby is a combined telephone kiosk and letter
box. These were quite common in the early 1900's, but Warrington's
is one of the few survivors. Also associated with the town are two
prominent entertainers: the television presenter Chris Evans was
born here, and the durable comedian and ukelele player George
Formby is buried in the town's cemetery.

Despite being located a mere two miles from Warrington and
little more than a mile from junction 21 of the M6, the **Paddington
House Hotel** is a wonderfully peaceful haven set in its own attractive grounds, complete with a tree-lined lawn and landscaped garden.

Paddington House Hotel

The oldest part of the house dates back to Georgian times, but it has been greatly extended since then and now provides 37 rooms, all en-suite, some with baths, some with showers, some with both.

The owners of the Paddington House Hotel, Robert and Rosemary Abson have a wealth of experience in the hotel and catering trade and certainly know how to look after their guests. Their philosophy is that a hotel should bring people through its doors for many different reasons. Good food, ales and wine, naturally, and you'll find those either in the cosy old bar area or in the stylish, intimate restaurant. Then there are the extensive conference facilities capable of seating parties of from eight to two hundred people. Throughout the year, the hotel hosts a series of special events - an Aintree weekend in April taking in the Grand National, an "Australian Christmas" dinner in June, and many others. You can even get married here. Paddington House is an Approved Building for civil weddings and offers a comprehensive package for the special event. *The Paddington House Hotel, Manchester Road, Warrington, WA1 3TZ. Tel: 01925 816767*

For visitors to the area looking for a place to stay, **Tall Trees Lodge**, just two and a half miles south of junction 10 off the M56, makes an ideal base from which to explore the surrounding Cheshire countryside. Opened in October 1992 by owners Denise and Paul Garnett, the modern exterior of this hotel belies the warm, friendly atmosphere within which makes this far and above the run of the mill lodge. The twenty en-suite guest rooms are attractively fur-

Tall Trees Lodge

nished and equipped to a high standard for maximum comfort, and the bar provides the perfect setting in which to relax with a quiet drink and light snack. With the Little Chef situated next door, you have ready access to full meals throughout the day, and travelling out a little way, you will find yourself within easy reach of many charming country pubs serving excellent food to suit all tastes. *Tall Trees Lodge, Tarporley Road, Lower Whitley, nr Warrington, WA4 4EZ. Tel: 01928 790824*

Around Warrington

Collins Green   Map 4 ref E1
5 miles NW of Warrington on the B5204
The Pear Tree Inn stands in the village of Collins Green. It's an impressive and substantial Victorian building which dates back to 1883 when it was built as The Station Hotel to service passengers on the Manchester to Liverpool line. It adopted its more appealing name around 1910 and is now a warm and friendly family pub run by Anne and Andy McKeever. Recently refurbished, The Pear Tree Inn is pleasingly decorated with lots of bygone memorabilia, pottery and ornaments.

The McKeevers serve really satisfying "pub grub" on weekday lunchtimes (noon - 2.30pm): hot dishes, sandwiches and desserts, all very reasonably priced. Children have their own menu, their own play area, and the proceeds from the Thursday Quiz Night are devoted to a party for children. There's free pool on Tuesday evenings, and every evening there's a really welcoming atmosphere. Since taking over in 1997, the McKeevers have won many new

The Pear Tree Inn

friends for The Pear Tree Inn. *The Pear Tree Inn, 1, Collins Green Lane, Collins Green, Burtonwood, Warrington, A5 4EQ. Tel: 01925 225749*

Risley
Map 4 ref F1

4 miles NE of Warrington on the A574

Parts of **The Noggin** pub, on the A574 between Warrington and Culcheth, date back to mid-Victorian times but this old hostelry is now one of the family of Greenalls popular pub/restaurants and has been stylishly refurbished. The attractively furnished, open plan interior with various raised levels creates an inviting impression, and parents will appreciate the large children's play area - and the fact that it is overlooked by the restaurant.

The Noggin

David and Yvonne Ingham have run The Noggin since 1996, maintaining very high standards of customer service: nowhere more so than in the restaurant, "Henrys Table", which particularly prides itself on its tender and succulent steaks, but whose menu also includes a wide choice of fish, chicken, pasta, and vegetarian dishes. The wine list offers a varied selection from around the world, available by the glass or bottle, and a separate dessert menu is an exercise in sheer indulgence. If you are just looking for a light meal, then you'll find an excellent bar snack menu available every day. *The Noggin, 687, Warrington Road, Risley, Warrington, WA3 6AY. Tel: 01925 812022*

Glazebrook
6 miles E of Warrington on the B5212
Map 4 ref G1

Set in its own pleasant gardens in a rural location, **The Rhinewood Inn & Hotel** is also conveniently situated close to the motorway network, just off junction 21 of the M6 and junction 2 of the M63, just along the A57 on the B5212. The accommodation here is particularly recommended. There are 32 bedrooms, half of them on the ground floor, all en-suite, and all comfortable and well-appointed with amenities such a remote control colour television and direct-dial telephone.

The Rhinewood Inn and Hotel

The restaurant offers both table d'hôte and à la carte menus, and there's a large friendly bar/lounge area where meals are also served. Children have their own blackboard menu and there are special deals for OAPs at lunchtime on Tuesday and Thursday. Since acquiring its licence to hold civil marriages, the Rhinewood Hotel's comprehensive package for the special event has enjoyed great popularity. Just contact them if you would like a copy of their wedding brochure which includes a "Wedding Timetable" providing a helpful countdown on how to plan all the complex arrangements. *The Rhinewood Inn & Hotel, Glazebrook Lane, Glazebrook, nr Warrington, WA3 5BB. Tel: 0161 775 5555*

A grand old farmhouse, built in 1851, stands at the heart of the **Mount Pleasant Farm Craft Centre** at Glazebrook. The converted old barns surrounding it house a huge variety of attractions with something to appeal to all the family. The popular Coffee Shop, with its quarry-tiled floor and welcoming log fire, offers an excellent choice of light meals, home made treats and daily specials and is attractively decorated with samples of the many quality crafts on sale in other parts of the complex. Toys, linen, jewellery, walking-sticks - the centre is brimming with gift ideas. The Craft Shop itself offers

Mount Pleasant Farm Craft Centre

an extensive range of gifts, crafts, knitwear and furnishings while the 3,000 sq. ft. conservatory furniture showroom displays the very latest in cane suites, occasional furniture and accessories. The Needlework Stable stocks every item a needlewoman could ever need and also arranges Embroidery Workshops about five times a month. In the Nursery Room, grandparents will find the perfect keepsake for a grandchild's christening day, birthday - or indeed any day. And yet another showroom is devoted to painted furniture along with dried and silk flowers, sold either in bunches or in ready-made basket arrangements. *Mount Pleasant Farm Craft Centre, Glazebrook, nr Warrington, WA3 5BN. Tel: 0161 775 2004*

Thelwall   Map 4 ref F2
3 miles E of Warrington on minor road off the A56

The history of **The Little Manor** in Thelwall village can be clearly traced back to 1737 when a Mr Thomas Percival bought the house for £25.00. The original deeds of that transaction were discovered in an old store cupboard when the inn was being renovated in 1973 and are now proudly displayed for customers to see. This historic old hostelry has been run by Colin and Jennifer Burne since 1991 and is one of the group of Greenalls "Henrys Table" pub/restaurants, offering customers stylish surroundings, an excellent choice of food, ales and wine, and first class service.

The Little Manor

The Little Manor is open all day, every day, with food available from noon - 2.30pm, and from 5.30-10pm, Monday to Saturday, and from noon until 10pm on Sunday. Children are allowed in selected areas, and access for the disabled is good, although the toilets are difficult. An additional attraction is the inn's lovely garden but ghost-hunters will be sorry to learn that a certain lady named Rachel who once haunted The Little Manor has not been seen for some years now. *The Little Manor, Bell Lane, Thelwall, Warrington, WA4 2SX. Tel: 01925 261703*

In and around Lymm

During the stage coach era, **Eagle Brow** was notorious, a dangerously steep road that dropped precipitously down the hillside into the village of Lymm. To bypass this hazard, a turnpike was built (now the A56), so preserving the heart of this ancient village with its half-timbered houses and well-preserved village stocks. The **Bridgewater Canal** flows past nearby and the church is reflected in the waters of **Lymm Dam**. Popular with anglers and bird-watchers, the dam is a large man-made lake, part of a lovely woodland centre which is linked to the surrounding countryside and the canal towpath by a network of footpaths and bridleways.

The village became an important centre for the fustian cloth (corduroy) trade in the 19th century but is now best known simply as a delightful place to visit. Lymm stands on the sides of a ravine and its streets have actually been carved out of the sandstone rock. The same rock was used to construct Lymm's best-known landmark, the ancient cross crowned with a huge cupola that stands at the top of the High Street.

For lovers of fine food, **The Lymm Bistro** can be found in an attractive 200 year old building and has been run for the past ten years by Jo Shenton and Michael Venning. Since opening the bistro, Jo and Michael have earned themselves an excellent reputation for providing first class food and wines. Michael is the chef and he has obviously gone to great lengths to ensure that his diners receive only the very best and freshest of produce. Meals are cooked to or-

Lymm Bistro

der and served in the cosy, friendly atmosphere which the bistro exudes. Michael's speciality is fish and this can be anything from a simple, but exquisite, whole Dover Sole to really exotic and exciting dishes. For example, it is not unknown for Michael to offer amongst his daily specials such unusual dishes as giant Australian Snow Crab, Fresh Lobster, or Parrot Fish. As one can imagine, offering dishes such as these makes the Lymm Bistro very popular and it is not surprising that diners travel from far and wide to sample such excellent cuisine.

Jo and Michael are on hand every evening to look after the personal requirements of their diners: the bistro also caters for special tastes, including vegetarian meals and private parties. Blackboard specials are always popular and a selection of starters may consist of king prawns Thai style with coriander, ginger, lemon grass and kaffir lime, or Monkfish wrapped in smoked bacon and grilled. The main courses are just as mouthwatering with such delights as fresh Marlin fish sautéed with various shellfish and served with a cream sauce, and wild boar, - a roast saddle of wild boar served in a sauce made from its own juices, juniper berries and port. As might be imagined, the Lymm Bistro does become extremely busy (it is best to book a table) and with a table d'hôte menu available during the week as well, represents superb value for money. *Lymm Bistro, 16, Bridgewater Street, Lymm, WA13 0AB. Tel: 01925 754852*

For more than fifty years **Willow Pool Garden Centre** and Nursery on Burford Lane at Lymm has been making life easy for the gardeners of Cheshire by providing them with a full range of healthy,

Willow Pool Garden Centre

attractive plants. Majestic magnolias, copious varieties of ivy, ever-greens, spring flowers and bedding plants are all available, many imported from Holland, Wales and Scotland. The Nursery and Garden Centre takes its name from the willow pool at its centre, a tranquil place surrounded by trees and graced with antique urns, pots and statuary. The owners of Willow Pool specialise in supplying these appealing garden ornaments and claim a 90% success rate in tracking down your own particular requirement: a vintage wrought iron pergola, perhaps, or an ornate garden table with accompanying chairs. A recent addition to the Willow Pool's attractions is its Tea Room. Its deep carpets and gleaming chandeliers provide a gracious setting in which to enjoy an extensive, up-market menu. *Willow Pool Garden Centre & Nursery, 25 Burford Lane, Lymm. Tel: 01925 757827 / Fax: 01925 758101*

Heatley

Map 4 ref G2

2 miles NE of Lymm on the A6144

The Green Dragon public house is an enchanting old building with white-painted walls adorned with hanging baskets of flowers. The interior has been completely refurbished but retains many of the old features: roaring open fires, wooden floors and beams decorated with bunches of dried flowers and lots of exposed brickwork along with an abundance of interesting bygones. Wooden benches, pews,

The Green Dragon

tables and chairs in many different styles add to the charm. Run by Steve Nugent, The Green Dragon has acquired a formidable reputation for its imaginative, attractively-priced menu which ranges from lighter lunches (such as a Mushroom, Cranberry & Courgette

Bake, or Game Pâté in Bard), to generous servings of steaks, pies, salads and mixed grill: "Great British food - all day every day" as the inn's motto puts it. Children are very welcome and in good weather can take advantage of the well-stocked play area outside. Disabled visitors will find ramps providing access to all the public areas and a disabled toilet - facilities that earned The Green Dragon an award from a national organisation for the disabled. *The Green Dragon, Mill Lane, Heatley, nr Lymm, WA13 9PM. Tel: 01925 750921*

Statham
Map 4 ref G2

3 miles NE of Lymm on minor road off the B6144

The Star Inn is very much the social centre of the tiny hamlet of Statham, near Lymm. It has its own football and darts teams, on Wednesday nights there's a very popular quiz, and Julia and Bernard Howarth have raised thousands of pounds for charities with auctions, occasional live entertainment, and an annual Fun Day. The inn itself is a listed building dating back to the early 1800's and has a warm and welcoming atmosphere with lots of old beams, a feature fireplace and attractive prints of old Statham and Lymm around the walls. Outside, there's a large beer garden, complete with bouncy castle.

The Star Inn

Good, straightforward "pub grub" - pies and sandwiches - is available throughout the day along with an excellent selection of fine cask ales in tip top condition. You get some idea of Julia and Bernard's qualities as "mine hosts" from the fact that Greenalls Breweries send new tenants here to train under their wing. Statham itself will fascinate anyone interested in the area's industrial heritage. The Manchester Ship Canal is just a short stroll away, the Bridgewater Canal even nearer, and the former Warrington to Manchester railway, now part of the Trans-Pennine Walk, is also close by. *The Star Inn, Star Lane, Statham, nr Lymm, WA13 9LN. Tel: 01925 753092*

Dunham Massey
Map 4 ref G2

6 miles E of Lymm on B5160

Tucked away in the scenic and historic village of Dunham Massey, **The Axe & Cleaver** is an attractive black and white building, part of the Chef & Brewer family of outstanding inns. Its history goes back to 1841 when it was a "Beer Shop" housed in a thatched cottage and run by "James Holt, Beer Seller". In summer, he would have opened as early as 5am so that farm labourers could fill their flagons before a day's work in the fields. Things have changed a bit since those times. Today's hosts at The Axe & Cleaver, Nick and

The Axe & Cleaver

Brigette Frankgate preside over elegantly furnished premises in olde worlde style with inviting cosy corners. Here they offer not just a fine selection of traditional ales but also a host of beautifully-prepared house specialities "served in belt-loosening portions!" The blackboard list is always changing and, if you just want something light, there's also an excellent choice of snacks and sandwiches (and even a Cream Tea). There are good facilities for the disabled, lovely gardens, and an off road car park. *The Axe & Cleaver, School Lane, Dunham Massey, Altrincham, WA14 5RN. Tel: 0161 928 3391*

Close by is **Dunham Massey Hall** and Park (National Trust). In its 250 acres of parkland, fallow deer roam freely, there's a restored water-mill which is usually in operation every Wednesday, and splendid walks in every direction. The Hall, once the home of the Earls of

Dunham Massey Hall

Stamford and Warrington, is a grand Georgian mansion of 1732 which boasts an outstanding collection of furniture, paintings and Huguenot silver. The Hall is open most days from April to October: the Park is open every day.

Moore   *Map 4 ref E2*
5 miles SW of Warrington on a minor road off the A56

Back in the 1600's, the village of Moore was just a scattering of a dozen farmhouses, one of which is now **The Red Lion** pub. A century later, when the Bridgewater Canal was being constructed close by, one enterprising villager decided to convert his house into a hostelry, and The Red Lion has been offering hospitality to locals and visitors ever since. Diane and Shaun McMahon now run this historic pub, an inviting place with an original Georgian frontage and, inside, low ceilings decked with dried hops and lots of bygone memorabilia around the walls, including fine old prints of local scenes.

Cask conditioned ales are always available and a guest beer cycle means there is a different guest beer available every week. The food served at The Red Lion is a special attraction. An excellent regular menu offers a wide choice of traditional meals, lite bites and

The Red Lion

sandwiches, while the specials board lists at least half a dozen more tasty options. (Bookings are strongly advised for Friday and Saturday evenings, and Sunday lunchtimes). On fairweather days, the beer garden and children's play area come into their own, and if you are a quiz devotee, make sure you're at The Red Lion on Wednesday night! *The Red Lion, Runcorn Road, Moore Village, nr Warrington, WA4 6UD. Tel: 01925 - 740205*

Daresbury
Map 4 ref E3

5 miles SW of Warrington on the A558

All Saints' Church in Daresbury has an absolutely unique stained glass window. There are panels depicting a Gryphon and a Cheshire Cat, others show a Mock Turtle, a March Hare and a Mad Hatter. This is of course the Lewis Carroll Memorial Window, commemorating the author of "Alice in Wonderland". Carroll himself is shown at one side, dressed in clerical garb and kneeling. His father was Vicar of Daresbury and he was born here in 1832 and baptised as Charles Lutwidge Dodgson. The boy enjoyed an apparently idyllic childhood at Daresbury until his father moved to another parish when Charles/Lewis was eleven years old.

Frodsham

Map 4 ref E3

10 miles NE of Chester on the A56

This is an attractive town with a broad High Street lined with thatched cottages and spacious Georgian and Victorian houses. During the 18th and early 19th centuries, Frodsham was an important coaching town and there are several fine coaching inns. Built in 1632, *The Bear's Paw* with its three stone gables recalls the bear-baiting that once took place nearby. Of the Earl of Chester's Norman castle only fragments remain, but the Church of St Laurence (an earlier church here was recorded in the Domesday Book) is noted for the fine 17th century panelling in its exquisite north chapel. The Vicar here from 1740 to 1756 was Francis Gastrell, a name that is anathema to all lovers of Shakespeare. Gastrell bought the poet's house, New Place, at Stratford and first incensed the towns-people by cutting down the famous mulberry tree. Then, in order to avoid paying the Corporation poor rate, he pulled the house itself down. The outraged citizens of Stratford hounded him from the town and he returned to the parish at Frodsham that he had neglected for years.

Anyone who lives in northwest Cheshire and loves Chinese food will already know Tony Yau's superb *Yuet Ben Restaurant* which he and his wife Sui Yung have owned and run since 1982. Newcomers to the area should seek it out, there's a real treat awaiting them. The Yuet Ben is housed in a listed building which, during the course of its long history, has served at various times as a school, an Army

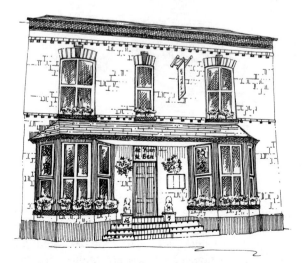

Yuet Ben Restaurant

canteen and even a retirement home. Since 1982, though, it has been Cheshire's premier location for sampling authentic Beijing cuisine, exquisitely prepared, beautifully presented, and served in opulent Oriental surroundings. The regular menu runs to more than a hundred different items, a marvellous selection of meat, poultry, seafood and vegetarian dishes. A sizzling platter of Prawns cooked Szechwan style, or a "Squirrel Fish" (Sweet & Sour Whole Trout); special set dinners for two or more people; a large range of tasty appetisers - these are just some of the options available. Should your preference be for vegan food, just give the Yaus prior notice and they can cater for that too. The Yuet Ben is open every evening. *Yuet Ben Restaurant, 64, Main Street, Frodsham, WA6 7AU. Tel: 01928 732232*

Standing on the main street of this beautiful village is the outstanding **Squires Restaurant**. Housed on the first floor of a Grade II listed building, the restaurant is beautifully decorated in rich, warm colours that create a relaxed and peaceful atmosphere. Michael Whalley, who has much experience of the catering business, opened Squires six years ago and has gained an excellent reputation for his

Squires Restaurant

glorious food. Open every day except Sunday, the restaurant is well known throughout the area. During the day, between 10am and 2pm, there is a tasty menu of snacks and light lunches that makes this a super meeting place. Come evening and the mood changes. The menu is extensive, with a host of special gourmet evenings throughout the year when diners can sample such delights as roasted quail filled with ostrich pâté, and wild boar steaks complemented by an orange, nutmeg and yoghurt sauce. Thursday night is Fish Night, incorporated with the â la carte menu. There is a choice of at least eight different varieties of fish fresh from the market that morning, plus a choice of 10 sauces to accompany the fish. In intimate and cosy surroundings guests can enjoy the very best of English, French and Italian cuisine, with all the dishes prepared to order. When a table is booked, it is for the evening, a final touch that makes a meal here the perfect dining experience. *Squires Restaurant, 4a High Street, Frodsham, WA6 7HE. Tel: 01928 735246*

As Confucius said, "To Live, To Eat...is to Live Well". His wise words are quoted on the menu of the **Chinese Delight Restaurant** which is, without doubt, one of the best Chinese restaurants not just in Cheshire, but in the whole of England. Attention to detail is paramount here: everything is constantly under the watchful eye of Eddie Chu, the genial proprietor. He personally supervises every aspect of the restaurant, even the quality of the ground coffee: twenty blends were tasted before one was found to meet Eddie's

Chinese Delight Restaurant

exacting standards. Visitors enter this outstanding restaurant by way of a bridge over an ornamental pond full of plump koi carp. Inside, the lavish oriental decor provides a perfect setting in which to enjoy the superlative cuisine which ranges from the meat-based dishes of Canton province to Hong Kong sea-food delicacies. A menu that covers a dozen closely-printed pages offers a huge range of choices: anything from an Emperor's Banquet for 4 or more diners, through a four-course Business Lunch, to a children's Sunday Banquet Lunch. The Chinese Delight Restaurant is understandably very popular, so it is always advisable to book your table well ahead. *Chinese Delight Restaurant, 15, Bridge Street, Frodsham, WA6 7HJ. Tel: 01928 733383. Fax: 01928 739292*

Helsby
Map 4 ref D4

8 miles NE of Chester on the A56

There are seven **Iron Age forts** scattered across Cheshire, but only the one at Helsby, maintained by the National Trust, is open to the public. The climb out of the village along pretty woodland paths to the red sandstone summit is quite steep but the views across the marshes to the Mersey Estuary and Liverpool repay the effort.

Housed in Helsby's Old Chapel, **Wonderland** offers a dazzling display of spectacular tropical and coldwater fish, a large selection of aquatic plants and, for anglers, a range of fishing gear and "consumables" such as bait. Carol and David McWilliaim's unusual centre is also known for it's wide choice of pets and xerophytes. Xerophytes? That's the botanical name for plants, which are able to withstand drought conditions - cacti, succulents and the like. A wide

Wonderland

range of them are stocked at various stages of maturity along with all the seeds, bulbs, composts, fertilisers and other aids required for successful indoor and outdoor gardening. There is an appealing assortment of small animals – hamsters, guinea pigs, chinchillas, mice, rabbits and birds along with just about every possible accessory to keep them happy and in good health. Cat and dog food, treats and toys, shampoos and treatments, beds, collars and leads, Wonderland has them all. Carol and David have combined their expertise to create this centre of aquatic and horticultural excellence. *Wonderland, The Old Chapel, Robin Hood Lane, Helsby, Cheshire, WA6 0EX. Tel: 01928 722774*

Elton

Map 1 ref D4

6 miles NE of Chester, off the A5117

Elton village is very conveniently located just a mile or so from junction 14 of the M56 and here you'll find **The Wheelwright Arms**, an inviting Free House with flagstone floors, low ceilings and many old beams. The owner, Ann Crosswaite has been in the licensed trade for some 20 years and at one time was a barmaid in this very pub which she now owns and runs with the help of her son Sean. Three

The Wheelwright Arms

houses make up the building, the central one dating back to the 1600's and with a cellar hewn out of the sandstone rock on which it stands. This is a very sociable pub, boasting its own football and darts teams, a pool table and a quiz night every Tuesday. The Wheelwright Arms is open all day, every day, with tasty (and very reasonably priced) bar snacks available throughout the day. The well-kept ales include Theakstons, Beamish, Fosters, and McKeowns amongst others and, although children are not allowed inside the pub, there's a pleasant beer garden at the rear where they are very welcome. *The Wheelwright Arms, Ince Lane, Elton, nr Chester, CH2 4LU. Tel: 01928 726444*

Ashton   *Map 1 ref D4*

8 miles E of Chester on the B5393

Just a short distance off the main A54 road, Ashton village is worth seeking out for the pleasure of visiting **The Golden Lion**. These 300-year-old premises, run by Jill and Brendan Phelan, are an absolute picture. Cosy, characterful rooms and open fires, - every detail of the decorations, furnishings, even the crockery and cutlery, is just as one would wish it. Food is available every day with no fewer than three separate menus: one for lunchtime, one for the evening, and one, the "Cubs Menu", for children. The Golden Lion's professional chefs offer an extensive choice of both light and hearty meals;

The Golden Lion

traditional favourites along with less familiar dishes such as kangaroo and antelope steaks. Evening meals are served until 9pm, Sunday to Thursday, 9.30pm on Friday and Saturday. An extremely popular part of the inn is the "Lion's Den", an inviting bar area, complete with a choice of real ales and a pool table. Wednesday is Quiz Night and for summer days there's an attractive, secluded beer garden to the rear of the inn. *The Golden Lion, Kelsall Road, Ashton Hayes, by Chester. Tel: 01829 751508*

A couple of miles to the northeast of Ashton stretch the 4,000 acres of **Delamere Forest**, a rambler's delight with a wealth of lovely walks and many picnic sites, ideal for a peaceful family day out. In Norman times, a "forest" was a part-wooded, part-open area, reserved as a hunting ground exclusively for royalty or the nobility. There were savage penalties for anyone harming the deer, even if the deer were destroying crops, and household dogs within the forest had to be deliberately lamed to ensure that they could not harass the beasts. James I was the last king to hunt deer here, in August 1617, and so enjoyed the day's sport that he made his Chief Forester a knight on the spot. Even at that date, many of the great oaks in the forest had already been felled to provide timber for ship-building, - as well as for Cheshire's familiar black and white half-timbered houses. Since the early 1900s, Delamere Forest has been maintained by the Forestry Commission which has undertaken an intensive programme of tree planting and woodland management. Delamere is now both an attractive recreational area and a working forest with 90% of the trees eventually destined for the saw mills.

Kingsley *Map 4 ref E4*
3 miles SE of Frodsham off the B5152, on the B5153

Just a mile or so north of Delamere Forest, in the village of Kingsley, is **The Horseshoe,** a friendly family pub run by Diana Wilbraham with the capable assistance of her daughters Jane and Kerry and with the help of Sandra and Steve – Steve also provides disco's for children's christmas parties as required. The Horseshoe is a spacious, Victorian-style house, dating back some 150 years when there

The Horseshoe

was good stabling here and the blacksmith next door was kept busy. At the time of going to press, The Horseshoe is not serving food but, by the time you read this, it may well be available. During the week, the pub opens at 5pm but at weekends it's also open from noon until 4pm. The well-kept ales include Greenalls Bitter and Mild, and Tetley's Smoothflow, and Diana keeps her customers entertained with something happening on most evenings. Wednesday is fund-raising night, for example, and on Saturday evenings there's live music from around 9.30pm. If you enjoy genuine old country pubs, the kind which are still very much the hub of village life, you will certainly appreciate The Horseshoe. *The Horseshoe, Hollow Lane, Kingsley, WA6 8EF. Tel: 01928 - 788466*

CHAPTER EIGHT
Northeast Cheshire

Bramall Hall

Chapter 8 - Area Covered

For precise location of places please refer to the colour maps found at the rear of the book.

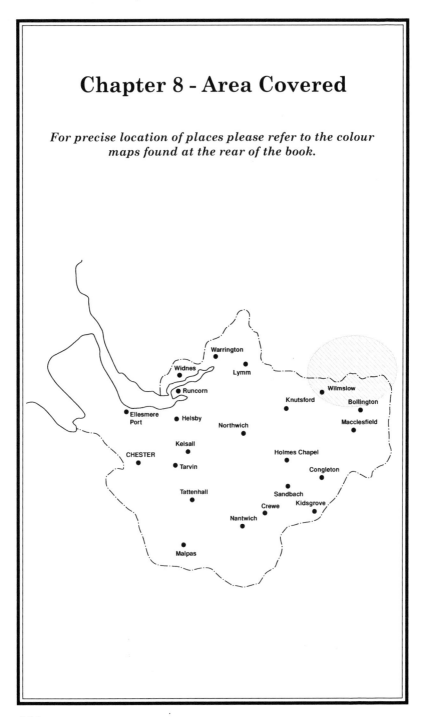

8
North East Cheshire

Altrincham

The writer Thomas de Quincey visited Altrincham in the early 1800's and thought its bustling market *"the gayest scene he ever saw"*. The market is still very active although the old houses that de Quincey also noted have sadly gone. A modern bustling town, Altrincham nevertheless has a long history with a charter granted in 1290 and clear evidence that there was a settlement beside the River Bollin some 6,000 years ago. Even older than that is the prehistoric body preserved in peat discovered on Lindow Common nearby. From Victorian times, Altrincham has been a favoured retreat for Manchester businessmen and the town is well-supplied with inns and restaurants.

In a convenient location near the town centre and close to the market, the *Oasis Coffee Shop* is an ideal place for a tea or coffee break. Barbara Hewitt has run the Oasis since 1989 and her welcoming coffee shop serves an excellent choice of beverages and light snacks, many of them costing well under a pound. It's difficult to think of anywhere else that provides such remarkable value for money.

The Oasis is non-smoking, and children and disabled are all welcome - there are a couple of steps but the friendly staff will happily give any assistance required. Upstairs, Tim Morris runs the shop which stocks a fine selection of Christian literature, tapes, CDs, gifts and cards. The coffee shop opens every day from 9.30am to 3pm, except Monday and Wednesday when it closes at 2pm. Definitely the place to seek out if you are looking for good, wholesome light

Oasis Coffee Shop

refreshment at an extremely reasonable price. The bookshop is open from Tuesday to Saturday. Both shops are closed on Sundays. *Oasis Coffee Shop, Charis House, 1, Central Way, Altrincham, WA14 1SB. Tel: 0161 928 1772*

Regent Road, in the heart of Altrincham, was known in the last century as *"The road that had nowt!"* Things have changed since then. For one thing, in Regent Road, at the corner of Central Way, is **Cousin Thelma's Coffee Shop**, an ideal place for a coffee break or a light meal. Genka Madylus has been running this bright and airy coffee shop since 1990 and her experience in providing wholesome, tasty food goes back beyond that. Nothing here is pre-cooked and most of the food on offer is home made.

The menu includes breakfast, oven baked potatoes, filled pancakes, salads, sandwiches, toasties and a kiddies' menu. There's a daily set menu of either two or three courses and you definitely shouldn't leave without trying one of the superb cakes or desserts. Understandably popular, Cousin Thelma's welcomes children, (even babies), and there's good access for the disabled. Just a couple of minute's walk from the Market and the town centre, Cousin Thelma's is open every day from 10am to 3.30pm. *Cousin Thelma's Coffee Shop, 18, Regent Road, Altrincham, WA14 1RP. Tel: 0161 941 1410*

Cousin Thelma's Coffee Shop

Bringing a touch of continental style to Hale village, ***Raison D'Etre*** offers all the amenities of a typical café-bar, serving good fresh coffee and tea along with excellent food every day between noon and 3pm. Wooden floors, stencilled walls, an ornate ceiling, soft background music, and the large, long bar all combine to create a very

Raison D'Etre

pleasing and distinctive ambience in this popular bar. The new lunchtime menu, just launched, includes hot sandwiches served on ciabatta, cold sandwiches and melts, old favourites like jackets and burgers, plus the introduction of combo's stir fries and Caffreys battered cod as main dishes. In addition, the blackboard lists side orders and some sumptuous desserts. Children are welcome and there's good access for wheelchairs. Raison D'Etre is open from 11.30am to 11pm, Monday to Saturday, and from noon until 10.30pm on Sunday. *Raison D'Etre, 173, Ashley Road, Hale, Altrincham, WA15 9SD. Tel: 0161 926 7951*

A mile or so further south, in the village of Ashley, you'll find **The Greyhound**. Family-run pubs always seem to have a particularly friendly atmosphere, and that's certainly true of The Greyhound. This four-square old house, dating back to the 17th century and attractively decked with hanging-baskets and tubs of flowers, is hosted by the Hayes family: Shaun and Julie, assisted by

The Greyhound

Emily and Ashley. Their pub was once part of the vast Egerton estates (the Egertons of Tatton Hall, the grandest house in Cheshire) and there are vibrant echoes of that aristocratic past in the olde worlde decorations and furnishings, and the roaring open fires.

At lunchtime, the main menu also harks back to those days, offering a comforting selection of hearty traditional meals, but you can also choose from a daily specials board and a selection of tasty snacks. In the evening, take your pick from either the traditional menu or from an imaginative list of à la carte dishes. Wine is sold by the glass or bottle, and the ale list encompasses Greenalls, Tetleys, Caffreys and other regular tipples. Children are welcome and are provided with their own large play area. *The Greyhound, Cow Lane, Ashley, nr Altrincham, WA15 0QR. Tel: 0161 941 2246*

Wilmslow

The oldest building in Wilmslow is **St Bartholomew's Church**, built between 1517 and 1537, and notable for its magnificent ceiling, some striking effigies, and for the fact that Prime Minister-to-be W. E. Gladstone worshipped here as a boy. A hamlet in medieval times, Wilmslow mushroomed as a mill town in the 18th and 19th centuries, and is now a busy commuter town offering a good choice of inns, hotels and restaurants.

Located close to the town centre, **The Farmers Arms** presents a very inviting appearance with its gleaming white walls and characterful windows. The interior is just as appealing. Open fires, old bench seats, a glittering array of copper and brass kettles and pots, two pianos, all combine to create a marvellous old world atmosphere. Landlady Ann Green, who has some 25 years experience

The Farmers Arms

as a licensee, took over here in 1997. Excellent, well-kept Boddington's ales, along with an extensive choice of other beers, are the speciality of the house, served with great style by barmaid Cynthia who has been here for more than 16 years. An extra attraction is planned for sometime during 1998, when Ann expects to start serving food at lunchtimes and in the evening. Built in the late 1800's, the Farmers Arms has lovely gardens at the rear with extra seating and a barbecue area. The pub is open all day, every day, children are welcome but the entrance steps make access for the disabled very difficult. *The Farmers Arms, 71, Chapel Lane, Wilmslow, SK9 5JH. Tel: 01625 532443*

The five acre site of **Ned Yates Garden Centre** in Moor Lane has been a nursery and seed trial grounds for many, many years but it takes its present name from Edward Yates who started The Ned Yates Walkround Nursery and Garden Store in 1965 and developed it into one of the finest garden centres in the county. It is now owned and run by the Jacques family who have continued Ned Yates' policy of providing a wide range of healthy, top-quality trees, shrubs and aquatic plants for both the professional and the amateur gardener.

Ned Yates Garden Centre

Their plants are very attractively displayed in the spacious grounds and if you have any questions of a horticultural nature, the experienced staff will be happy to provide advice and the centre also offers a landscape gardening service. As for garden accessories, from seeds to tools, composts to garden sheds, you'll find a comprehensive display of everything you could possibly need to make your garden the envy of the neighbourhood. An additional attraction is the beautifully-decorated Coffee Shop offering a good choice of beverages, cakes and light meals every day of the week. *Ned Yates Garden Centre, Moor Lane, Wilmslow, SK9 6DN. Tel: 01625 522128 / Fax: 01625 536377*

There aren't all that many places in England where you can sample Armenian cuisine so Wilmslow is very lucky in having the **Alcazar Restaurant** on its doorstep, just a few minutes walk from the town centre. Sarkis Srabonian was the first to bring the exotic,

Alcazar Restaurant

subtly-flavoured dishes of his native land to the north-west, first to Manchester, and then in 1987 to Wilmslow where his son, Hovsep, now presides over this understandably popular restaurant. Hovsep offers a fascinating menu with each dish accompanied by a helpful description: Faruj, for example, is "marinated roasted chicken stuffed with spicy minced lamb, rice and nuts, served with a brandy sauce". Tasty soups and starters, hearty meat and fish kebabs, rice "prepared with angel hair", cous-cous dishes and rich desserts (or a simple bowl of green figs): the Alcazar offers a unique eating experience. If your exploration of Cheshire takes you anywhere near Wilmslow, make sure you seek out this truly unique restaurant. *Alcazar Restaurant, 102, Water Lane, Wilmslow, SK9 5DB. Tel: 01625 526855*

Annette and Jerry Chalmers' **Finney Green Cottage** is a very special place for bed and breakfast - a lovely black and white, timber-framed house set in secluded leafy gardens. This Grade II listed building was originally built as a yeoman's residence in the early 1500's, altered and extended over the years to meet increased expectations of comfort, but with a wealth of charming old features still in place. There are old beams everywhere, a fire-window in the ingle-nook, a rare diamond-mullion oak window in the hall, and a

Finney Green Cottage

splendidly decorative 17th century cast iron fireback bearing King Charles' initials in the parlour. The three double rooms are all attractively furnished and overlook the peaceful garden with its feature well. Two are en-suite, the third has its own private bathroom. Breakfast is served in the original hall of the house and guests are welcome to relax in the adjoining sitting-room which also has views across the garden. Children are welcome, but because of the great age of the house, smoking is not permitted. *Finney Green Cottage, 134, Manchester Road, Wilmslow, SK9 2JW. Tel: 01625 533343*

The Chilli Banana brings an authentic taste of exotic Thai cuisine to the busy little town of Wilmslow. May Wakefield, who together with her husband, Steve, runs this outstanding restaurant, comes from Thailand and so do the experienced staff of cooks and waitresses. So you can be sure that you are getting the genuine article when you order a Tod Man Pla (spicy Thai fish cakes) as a starter, for example, or a Eung Kratiem (prawns stir-fried with garlic) as a main course. Some of the recipes have been handed on to May by her relatives in Thailand: the ingredients are kept secret but there's no concealing the fact that the results are truly

The Chilli Banana

delicious. In the best Thai tradition, service is gracious, courteous and friendly. Although the Chilli Banana only opened in March 1997, it has already attracted a dedicated clientele who return again and again, so booking is advisable at all times and essential on Saturday evenings. The restaurant is open at lunchtimes until 3pm, evenings until 11pm, but is closed on Mondays. A take-away service is also available. *The Chilli Banana, Kings Arms Hotel, Alderley Road, Wilmslow, SK9 1PZ. Tel: 01625 539100*

Since at least 1934, gardeners have been making their way to the *Morley Nursery*, a mile and a half or so outside Wilmslow, in search of interesting and unusual plants, shrubs and trees for their gardens and conservatories. Julie Tudor, who took over this long established nursery in 1976, has maintained and enhanced the Morley Nurseries' reputation for high quality plants of every description. This is very much a "plant persons" nursery, a "Gardeners'

Morley Nursery

World" of its own, run by knowledgeable and helpful staff. There is good wheelchair access and ample parking space. The nursery offers a comprehensive range of plants, - if it's possible to grow something in Cheshire, you'll almost certainly find a good example of it here. But Julie also specialises in cultivating unusual indoor and outdoor specimens, and plants ideally suited for conservatories - Mediterranean shrubs and flowers, orange and lemon trees, mimosas and exotic flowering plants, and much more. Other specialities include field-grown Leylandii and conifers. *Morley Nursery, Altrincham Road, Wilmslow. Tel: 01625 528953*

Styal

Map 3 ref H3

1 mile N of Wilmslow, on a minor road off the B5166

Mark Moss and his mother Lynda took over the **Styal Chop House** just a few years ago and in that short time their reputation for excellent, home-cooked food has spread far and wide in the Cheshire area. The restaurant is quite small, seating about 40 on two levels, and this creates a wonderful atmosphere, more like Grandma's parlour than a restaurant. The artefacts and memorabilia on the walls

Styal Chop House

and shelves provide some interesting talking points and there is a curious collection of vintage tins. The menu offers all the traditional dishes you would wish to find in an English chop house and is supplemented by a daily specials board. Everything is cooked to order, allowing time for an aperitif or glass of wine from the exciting wine list. Do leave room for a pudding: they are all home made and just like the ones mother used to make. The Styal Chop House is open for lunch and dinner every weekday except Monday, and on Sundays from noon until 4pm when there's a special 2-course lunch at a very reasonable set price. *Styal Chop House, Altrincham Road, Styal, SK9 4JE. Tel: 01625 548144*

Cared for by the National Trust, **Styal Country Park** is set in 250 acres of the beautifully wooded valley of the River Bollin and offers many woodland and riverside walks. The Park is open to the public from dawn to dusk throughout the year and is a wonderful place for picnics. Lying within the Park is **Quarry Bank Mill**, a grand old building erected in 1784 and one of the first generation of cotton mills. It was powered by a huge iron waterwheel fed by the River Bollin. Visitors follow the history of the mill through various galleries and displays within the museum, including weaving and spinning demonstrations, and can experience for themselves, with the help of guides dressed in period costume what life was like for the hundred girls and boys who once lived in the Apprentice House. The Mill has a shop and a restaurant and is open every day from April to September from 11am to 6pm, and from October to March every day except Monday from 11am to 5pm (last entries 90 minutes before closing time).

Also within the park is the delightful **Styal Village** which was established by the mill's original owner, Samuel Greg, a philanthropist and pioneer of the factory system. He took children from the slums of Manchester to work in his mill, and in return for their labour provided them with food, clothing, housing, education and a place of worship.

Woodford
Map 3 ref I3
3 miles NE of Wilmslow on the A5102
Barton Grange Garden Centre is one of three identically named garden centres in the area, all of them established by Eddie Topping and all named after the first one he opened at Barton near Preston in 1963. This one, in the attractive village of Woodford covers more than 13 acres and it really does have everything for the keen amateur or ardent professional gardener. It is well laid out, with plenty of greenhouses to wander through, and you don't have to be a gardener to appreciate the magnificent plants on display, all covered by Barton's "guaranteed to grow" promise. The centre also

Barton Grange Garden Centre

stocks everything from tools and fertilisers, right through to garden furniture, water features, pets, and also offers an award-winning landscaping service. From October to December, you'll find a spectacular range of Christmas decorations and gift ideas which has to be seen to be believed. An additional attraction at Barton's is the Farmhouse Restaurant which serves a wonderful breakfast, luncheon and afternoon tea menu and caters for all ages. Both the garden centre and the restaurant are open every day, all year. Barton Grange Garden Centre, Chester Road, Woodford, SK7 1QS. Tel: 0161 439 0745

Just a couple of miles from Woodford is one of the grandest old "magpie" houses in Cheshire, **Bramall Hall**. This eye-catching, rambling perfection of black and white timbered buildings overlooks some 62 acres of exquisitely-landscaped woods, lakes and formal gardens. The oldest parts of the Hall date from the 14th century: for five of the next six centuries it was owned by the same family, the Davenports. Over the years, the Davenport family continually altered and extended the originally quite modest manor house. But

Bramall Hall

whenever they added a new Banqueting Hall, "Withdrawing Room", or even a Chapel, they took pains to ensure that its design harmonised happily with its more ancient neighbours. Along with Little Moreton Hall and Gawsworth Hall, Bramall represents the fullest flowering of a lovely architectural style whose most distinctive examples are all to be found in Cheshire.

Adlington   *Map 3 ref I3*
4 miles N of Macclesfield off the A523

The village of Adlington can also boast a fine old house. **Adlington Hall** has been the home of the Legh family since 1315 and is now one of the county's most popular attractions. Quadrangular in shape, this magnificent manor house has two distinctive styles of architecture: black and white half-timbered buildings on two sides, later

Adlington Hall

Georgian additions in warm red brick on the others. There is much to see as you tour the hall, with beautifully polished wooden floors and lovely antique furnishings enhancing the air of elegance and grandeur. The Great Hall is a breathtaking sight, a vast room of lofty proportions that set off perfectly the exquisitely painted walls. The beautifully-preserved 17th century organ here has responded to the touch of many maestros, none more famous than George Frederick Handel who visited the Hall in the 1740's.

It wasn't long after Handel's visit to Cheshire that the county was gripped by a mania for building canals, a passion that has left Cheshire with a uniquely complex network of these environment-friendly waterways. **Ken's Canalside Café**, located in the Lyme View Marina at Adlington, provides a welcome stopping off place for travellers along the Macclesfield Canal; for walkers following the towpath; and indeed for anyone exploring the countryside around

Ken's Canalside Café

Macclesfield. It's a smart new building where children are welcome, access for the disabled is made easy, smokers have their own area and an attractive patio beckons you outside on warm days. Alison Bonner presides over this family business with her Mum and Dad, Cynthia and Richard, on hand to help at busy times.

The day starts with a "Big Barge Special" breakfast (available all day, in fact), followed by a "Mid-Morning Break" (a hot toasted teacake, perhaps) and then comes "Alison's Main Menu" of hearty, home made meals and irresistible desserts, a menu which always includes a couple of vegetarian dishes and a selection of children's meals. For smaller appetites, there's also a choice of freshly made sandwiches and toasties available throughout the day. River and waterside eating places always seem to have a particular appeal, and Ken's Canalside Café certainly has this charm in abundance. *Ken's Canalside Café, Wood Lane East, Adlington, Macclesfield, SK10 4PH. Tel: 01625 850985*

The "Panhandle"

This narrow finger of land pointing up to West Yorkshire was chopped off from Cheshire in the 1974 Local Government redrawing of boundaries, but a quarter of a century later most of its population still consider themselves Cheshire folk. At its northern end lie Longdendale and Featherbed Moss, Pennine scenery quite unlike anywhere else in the county. Visitors to Cheshire tend to overlook this orphaned quarter: we strongly recommend that you seek it out.

Mellor
Map 3 ref J2

4 miles E of Marple on minor road off the A626

The village of Mellor, just a mile or so from the edge of the Peak District National Park, is a typical Cheshire village and well-provided with that most essential ingredient of village life, a good old-fashioned village pub, **The Royal Oak**. Les Smith has been "mine host" here for a remarkable 31 years, assisted since 1996 by his son, Sam. The pub itself, however, has an even longer history. It was

The Royal Oak

formerly part of a row of cottages built some 300 years ago and converted into a hostelry fifty years later. Inside, the old beams, stone floor and real fires are all still in place, supplemented now by paintings and prints by local artists and vintage memorabilia. The Royal Oak doesn't serve food, the speciality here is the ale. Robinson's Best Bitter and Hatters Mild are the star brews, served along with a good choice of other popular favourites. For fair weather days, there's a charming patio and beer garden to the rear where children are welcome, and most Thursday evenings are Quiz Nights. *The Royal Oak, Longhurst Lane, Mellor, Stockport, SK6 5PJ. Tel: 0161 427 1655*

Mottram
Map 3 ref K1

4 miles NE of Hyde on the A628

Mottram village is set on a breezy hillside on the edge of the Pennines. According to the 1930's guide-book writer Arthur Mee, the off-Atlantic gusts that scour the village are known locally as Captain Whitle's Wind. In the 16th century, the story goes, coffin-bearers carrying the late Captain were struggling up the steep hill to the church when gale-force winds swept the coffin from their shoulders.

Broadbottom
Map 3 ref K1

3 miles SE of Hyde on minor road off the A560

There are many pubs in England called **The Station**, but very few so close to the track as the one you'll find on the platform of Broadbottom Station, on the line between Hadfield and Manchester. It used to be the Station Master's house and was built around 1840, but is now a much more inviting place. Linda Grogan took over here in 1997, completely refurbished the interior and now offers food which gives a whole new meaning to the concept of "railway catering". There are two superb eating areas: The Gallery, which

The Station

overlooks the main bar area, and the no-smoking Pullman Restaurant, furnished in the same style as those vintage, luxury carriages and offering the same kind of quality, à la carte, meals. The Station is a free house, so in addition to the excellent food, you'll also find a wide choice of regular and guest beers, and entertainments include a folk night every Wednesday. Children are welcome (with a free lunch on Sunday for each under-12 looking after an adult), and there's full access for the disabled. Linda Grogan has created a very special hostelry here, so whether you are travelling by car or by train through Longdendale, make absolutely sure you alight at this particular Station. *The Station, Mottram Road, Broadbottom, via Hyde. Tel: 01457 766734*

Matley
Map 3 ref K1

Just S of Stalybridge on the A383

Just half a mile out of Stalybridge stands **The Dog & Partridge**. This sturdy old house with its attractive leaded windows and white railings dates back to the 18th century when it was built as the flagship pub for the independent Garside Brewery on the other side of the road. The brewery has closed long since but The Dog & Partridge remains a flagship for its real ales (Worthington and Stones,

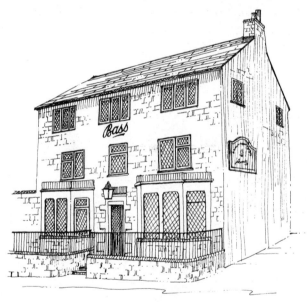

The Dog and Partridge

plus a guest beer) and its first class food. There's a wonderful atmosphere in this traditional inn with its many old beams, brass floor to ceiling pillars and a wealth of interesting features like the display of model vintage ships. Samantha Farrell is your welcoming host, her fiancé Michael Rogers is in charge of the kitchen where he prepares hearty meals such as home made Steak & Kidney Pie, pastas, steaks, and chicken and fish dishes. In addition, there are always four or five main course specials every day, available lunchtime and evenings Monday to Friday, and all day at weekends. If you're visiting on a Monday evening, feel free to join in the Quiz Night starting about 9.30pm. *The Dog & Partridge, 383, Mottram Road, Matley, Stalybridge, SK15 2SX. Tel: 01457 762153*

Tourist Information Centres

Centres in **bold** are open all the year around.

Altrincham
Stamford New Road, Altrincham, Cheshire WA14 1EJ
Tel: 0161 912 5931, Fax: 0161 941 7089

Birkenhead
Woodside Visitors Centre, Woodside Ferry Terminal, Birkenhead,
Merseyside L41 6DU
Tel: 0151 647 6780, Fax: 0151 666 2448

Chester
Town Hall, Northgate Street, Chester, Cheshire, CH1 2HJ
Tel: 01244 402385, Fax: 01244 400420

Congleton
Town Hall, High Street, Congleton, Cheshire, CW12 1BN
Tel: 01260 271095, Fax: 01260 298243

Knutsford
Council Offices, Toft Road, Knutsford, Cheshire, WA16 6TA
Tel: 01565 632611, Fax: 01565 652367

Macclesfield
Macclesfield Borough Council, Council Offices, Town Hall,
Macclesfield, Cheshire, SK10 1DX
Tel: 01625 504114

Nantwich

Church House, Church Walk, Nantwich, Cheshire, CW5 5RG
Tel: 01270 610983

Warrington

21 Rylands Street, Warrington, Cheshire, WA1 1EJ
Tel: 01925 442180, Fax: 01925 442149

Index

The Hidden Places Series

ORDER FORM

To order more copies of this title or any of the others in this series
please complete the order form below and send to:

**Travel Publishing Ltd,7a Apollo House, Calleva Park
Aldermaston, Berkshire, RG7 8TN**

	Price	Quantity	Value
Regional Titles			
Channel Islands	£6.99	....	....
Cheshire	£6.99	....	....
Devon & Cornwall	£4.95	....	....
Dorset, Hants & Isle of Wight	£4.95	....	....
East Anglia	£4.95	....	....
Gloucestershire	£6.99	....	....
Heart of England	£4.95	....	....
Lancashire	£7.99	....	....
Lake District & Cumbria	£7.99	....	....
Northeast Yorkshire	£6.99	....	....
Northumberland & Durham	£6.99	....	....
Nottinghamshire	£6.99	....	....
Peak District	£6.99	....	....
Potteries	£6.99	....	....
Somerset	£6.99	....	....
South East	£4.95	....	....
South Wales	£4.95	....	....
Surrey	£6.99	....	....
Sussex	£6.99	....	....
Thames & Chilterns	£5.99	....	....
Welsh Borders	£5.99	....	....
Wiltshire	£6.99	....	....
Yorkshire Dales	£6.99	....	....
Set of any 5 Regional titles	**£25.00**	....	....
National Titles			
England	£9.99	....	....
Ireland	£8.99	....	....
Scotland	£8.99	....	....
Wales	£8.99	....	....
Set of all 4 National titles	**£28.00**	....	....
TOTAL			

**For orders of less than 4 copies please add £1 per book for
postage & packing. Orders over 4 copies P & P free.**

PLEASE TURN OVER TO COMPLETE PAYMENT DETAILS

The Hidden Places Series
ORDER FORM

Please complete following details:

I wish to pay for this order by:

Cheque: ☐   Switch: ☐

Access: ☐   Visa: ☐

Either:

Card No: ☐☐☐☐ ☐☐☐☐ ☐☐☐☐ ☐☐☐☐

Expiry Date: ☐☐ ☐

Signature: ....

Or:

I enclose a cheque for £ .... made payable to Travel Publishing Ltd

NAME: ....

ADDRESS: ....

....

....

....

POSTCODE: ....

TEL NO: ....

Please send to: Travel Publishing Ltd
7a Apollo House
Calleva Park
Aldermaston
Berkshire, RG7 8TN

The Hidden Places Series
READER REACTION FORM

The Hidden Places research team would like to receive reader's comments on any visitor attractions or places reviewed in the book and also recommendations for suitable entries to be included in the next edition. This will help ensure that the **Hidden Places** series continues to provide its readers with useful information on the more interesting, unusual or unique features of each attraction or place ensuring that their stay in the local area is an enjoyable and stimulating experience.

To provide your comments or recommendations would you please complete the forms below as indicated and send to: **The Research Department, Travel Publishing Ltd., 7a Apollo House, Calleva Park, Aldermaston, Reading, RG7 8TN.**

Please tick as appropriate: Comments ☐ Recommendation ☐

Name of *"Hidden Place"*:

Address:

Telephone Number:

Name of Contact:

Comments/Reason for recommendation:

Name of Reader:

Address:

Telephone Number:

Map Section

The following pages of maps encompass the main cities, towns and geographical features of Cheshire, as well as all the many interesting places featured in the guide. Distances are indicated by the use of scale bars located below each of the maps

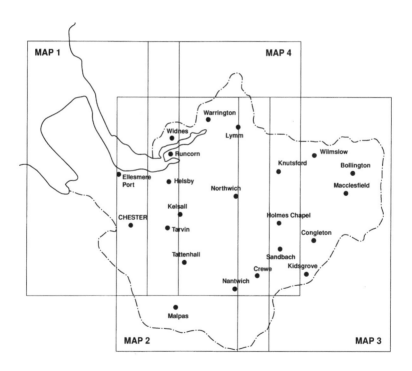

These maps are small scale extracts from the *North West England Official Tourist Map,* reproduced with kind permission of *Estates Publications.*

MAP 1

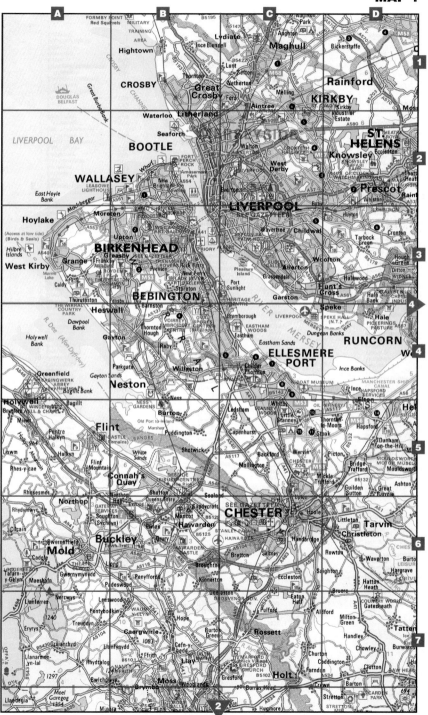

195

MAP 2

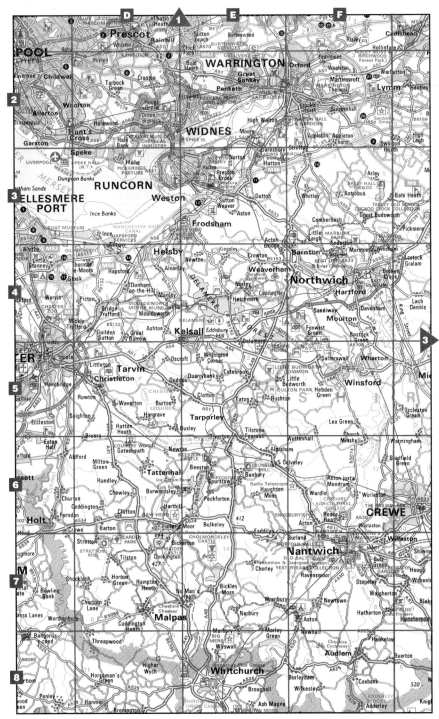

MAP 3

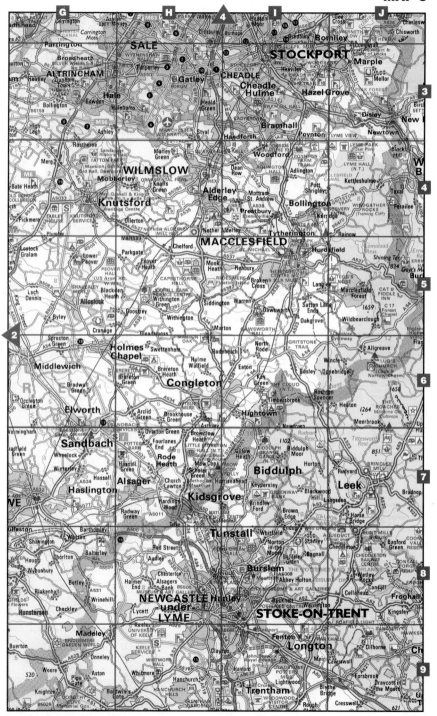

0   1   2   3   4   5 miles
0 1 2 3 4 5 6 7   8 kilometres

MAP 4

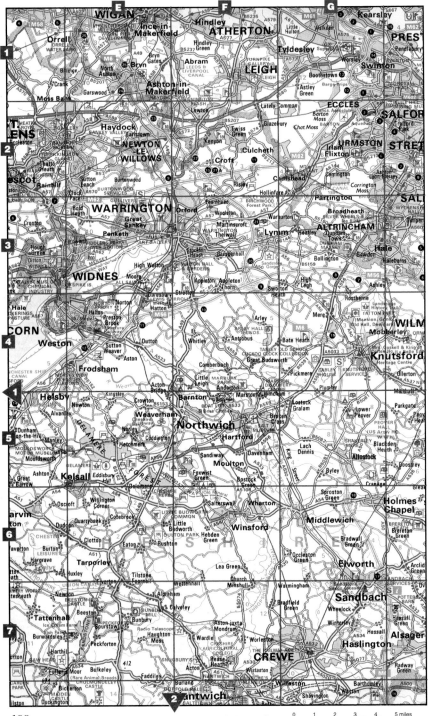

©Estate Publications   Crown Copyright Reserved

0 1 2 3 4 5 miles
0 1 2 3 4 5 6 7 8 kilometres